ANIMAL FARM

NOTES

COLES EDITORIAL BOARD

Bound to stay open

Publisher's Note

Otabind (Ota-bind). This book has been bound using the patented Otabind process. You can open this book at any page, gently run your finger down the spine, and the pages will lie flat.

ABOUT COLES NOTES

COLES NOTES have been an indispensible aid to students on five continents since 1948.

COLES NOTES are available for a wide range of individual literary works. Clear, concise explanations and insights are provided along with interesting interpretations and evaluations.

Proper use of COLES NOTES will allow the student to pay greater attention to lectures and spend less time taking notes. This will result in a broader understanding of the work being studied and will free the student for increased participation in discussions.

COLES NOTES are an invaluable aid for review and exam preparation as well as an invitation to explore different interpretive paths.

COLES NOTES are written by experts in their fields. It should be noted that any literary judgement expressed herein is just that — the judgement of one school of thought. Interpretations that diverge from, or totally disagree with any criticism may be equally valid.

COLES NOTES are designed to supplement the text and are not intended as a substitute for reading the text itself. Use of the NOTES will serve not only to clarify the work being studied, but should enhance the reader's enjoyment of the topic.

Animal Farm, by George Orwell.
First published in Great Britain in 1945
by Martin Secker & Warburg Limited
©1945 Estate of Eric Blair

ISBN 0-7740-3679-6

© COPYRIGHT 1991 AND PUBLISHED BY
COLES PUBLISHING COMPANY
TORONTO—CANADA
PRINTED IN CANADA

Manufactured by Webcom Limited
Cover finish: Webcom's Exclusive **Duracoat**

CONTENTS

George Orwell: Life and Works

George Orwell, whose real name was Eric Blair, was born in 1903, in Bengal, India, the son of a minor official in the Indian Civil Service. As was customary, his mother brought him, along with his two sisters, back to England when he was eight to be educated.

Orwell was sent to a boarding school on the South Coast, a school whose students were largely sons of the wealthy. To attract such students, the school concentrated mainly on "cramming" boys for entrance to Harrow and Eton. Orwell was one of a few bright boys allowed to attend at a lower tuition, a practice followed to ensure the winning of scholarships for the honor of the school. He came from what he himself called the "lower-upper-middle class" and hence was subjected to the snobbery of the other boys and the headmaster and his wife. He would later write that the psychological pressure set his mind for life and, although many critics now feel that he tended to adopt poses in his autobiographical writing, the situation must have been oppressive for a sensitive child.

Orwell went to Eton in 1917 on a scholarship. The atmosphere was freer there, he made friends, and he read a good deal. He also encountered, for the first time, popular liberal and socialist ideas. Such ideas were common subjects of discussion at Eton, especially in this period immediately following World War I. When he graduated in 1921, he decided not to go on to a university, though he could have. Instead, he joined the civil service and went to Burma as a sergeant in the Indian Imperial Police.

Orwell served in Burma from 1922 to 1927. As a policeman, he was, of course, the embodiment of British imperialism to the natives, a painful reversal of roles in comparison to his life as a schoolboy. He intensely disliked being the instrument by which power was exercised over the Burmese; on the other hand, he had to play the part of one in authority. When he returned to England on leave in 1927, he resigned his post.

For various reasons, not all of them clear even to Orwell himself, he then deliberately chose to live among poor working people in Paris and among tramps in England for more than a year. These experiences formed the basis for his first book, an autobiographical work he called *Down and Out in Paris and London,* published in 1933. Although he had published some early writing under his real name, the first book used the name "George Orwell." He later explained that he took the last name from an English river near which he had once lived and the first as typically English. In any case, it was probably a symbolic act signalling his choice of vocation as well as his attitude toward his own country.

During these years he worked as a teacher and, after he married, he and his wife kept a village tavern and general store. His income was small, and his first book brought him very little success. His first novel, *Burmese Days*, based on his experiences in Burma, came out in 1934. In 1935, he published another novel, *A Clergyman's Daughter*, which makes use, in part, of his teaching experience.

Although by now he had received critical comment in a few places, he was not making enough income from his writing to depend on it entirely. The novel, *Keep the Aspidistra Flying*, published in 1936, was based on his experiences at this time as a clerk in a bookstore. He became an active socialist during this period and, when his publisher encouraged him to visit a depressed industrial area and write about his personal reactions, he took the opportunity to put his political convictions into action. The results of his trip, *The Road to Wigan Pier*, came out in 1937.

Meanwhile, the Spanish Civil War had broken out and, though Orwell went as an observer and reporter, he soon enlisted on the Republican side. By chance, he joined a militia loyal to the P.O.U.M. (*Partido Obrero de Unificación Marxista* — Workers' Party of Marxist Unification), a Marxist but anti-Stalinist political party, rather than the better known (at least in America at the time) International Brigade, which was ultimately communist-controlled. He was badly wounded on the front, and by the time he recovered from the wound, the Republican government was dominated by communist groups responsive to direction from Russia, and the purge of other political parties, including the P.O.U.M., was under way. Orwell and his wife were forced to leave Spain for fear of imprisonment and possible summary execution. What he saw in Spain shocked him badly. He believed the communists' actions there had betrayed a popular revolution that might otherwise have given the working classes true freedom and status. The book he wrote from his Civil War experience, *Homage to Catalonia*, published in 1938, reflected this idea of the revolution betrayed, an idea that would find its ultimate form in *Animal Farm*.

Upon his return to England, Orwell published another novel, *Coming Up for Air*, in 1939. This was the first of his books to sell at all well. The war, which he had predicted in this book, was soon under way and, although he tried to enter the army, he was rejected for service because of the tuberculosis from which he suffered all his life. He was accepted in the Home Guard, however, and during World War II he also worked for a time in the Indian Service of the British Broadcasting Corporation.

Two collections of essays, *Inside the Whale, and Other Essays* and *The Lion and the Unicorn: Socialism and the English Genius*, appeared in 1940 and 1941. In addition, during this time, Orwell did a great deal of political journalism. A regular column, ''As I Please,'' appeared in the *London Tribune*; and he contributed to the *Observer, Manchester Evening News, Partisan Review* and *New Leader*.

In 1945, Orwell published the first of the two books for which he is generally known, *Animal Farm*. An anti-utopian novel, like *1984*, it is cast in the form of an animal satire. The obvious subject of the satire is Soviet Russia, but more generally it has to do with totalitarianism of any kind. The success of the book in Great Britain and the United States gave Orwell an income he had never before enjoyed.

Dickens, Dali, and Others, another collection of essays, appeared in 1946. With the death of his wife in the same year, Orwell had the complete care of his adopted son. In order to find the time to complete a book which embodied the ideas that concerned him most at this time, he moved to the Scottish Hebrides. His most celebrated book, *1984*, was published in 1949 In it, Orwell represents a near-future society that is an ominous projection of totalitarianism in the contemporary world. Although he remarried and was planning new work for the future, he died in London, in early 1950, from poor health and exhaustion.

Two other collections of essays appeared shortly after his death: *Shooting an Elephant, and Other Essays*, in 1950, and *Such, Such Were the Joys*, in 1953.

Orwell, Communism and Socialism

It is impossible to appreciate Orwell's work fully without understanding his political views, yet, in North America especially, students often misunderstand them. Many are surprised to learn that, although he was an outspoken anti-communist, he was also an ardent socialist all his life.

The failure to distinguish between socialism and communism causes the confusion. Socialism refers generally to any economic system based on the ownership of goods and property collectively (by all or a large part of society) rather than by individuals. The idea was described at least as early as Plato's *Republic* (fourth century B.C.) and was practised by the early Christians. In its modern forms, those developed from the 1830s on, socialism preaches government ownership of goods and control of their production and distribution. It does not usually insist on the abolition of private property, though it seeks to regulate this insofar as it affects public interests. Many variations of socialist beliefs and practice exist.

Communism is a specific form of socialism, developed from principles laid down by Karl Marx and Friedrich Engels in the *Communist Manifesto* (1847) and *Das Kapital* (1867–94). Although recent decades have seen some variations arise in its methods and politics, it always seeks the abolition of private property. And it advocates, at least in theory, the wresting of ownership, production and control of goods by violent revolution. Socialists, on the other hand, seek to obtain the means of production by legal and relatively peaceful means.

Socialism has a long and respected tradition in Great Britain and many parts of Europe, where it has attracted the allegiance of many thinkers and artists, as well as politicians, for well over a century. In mild forms, it is often the policy of legitimate political parties and democratically elected governments.

Since about the 1890s, many of Great Britain's intelligentsia have been socialists; indeed, during the 1920s through the 1940s socialism was almost the norm in many artistic circles. Surely, they thought, there must be a better way of organizing a world that was suffering the aftermath of World War I, growing industrialization, the great Depression (and several smaller, earlier ones), the rise of fascism and the bitter Spanish Civil War. There was much disagreement about specifics, however, and great theoretical battles were waged among the literary adherents of various schools of thought.

One problem for these Western socialists was how to react to communism as it was evolving in Soviet Russia after the Revolution of 1917. It was, at that time, the only government in the world based on completely socialistic principles, and many socialists elsewhere felt they had to give it some support, even if they disagreed with part of its theoretical basis. As history unfolded, Soviet propaganda, secrecy and isolation made it difficult for others even to know what was going on in

Russia. Rumors drifted out, but they were just that — rumors. It is difficult for us to realize today that until the 1950s the world did not know the truth about the outrages committed by Stalin or the shape communism had taken. And, when the Soviet Union entered World War II on the Allied side, many people thought that it might be better not to know, or that communism's opposition to fascism was so important as to be worth ignoring other facets of the theory and its practice.

Orwell disagreed, as he showed in writing *Animal Farm* and then *1984*. But he had been disagreeing with many other socialists for much of his adult life. Even before he wrote these books, much of his writing, especially his essays and newspaper articles, had involved criticism of socialism as well as advocacy of it.

Early on, he had insisted that it was necessary for socialism to separate itself from utopian idealism, arguing that although socialism was the only hope of the world, it could not claim to make society perfect. He had also directed much criticism at the socialist British Labour Party, claiming that it preached not genuine socialism, which should be concerned with the welfare of all people, but only the advancement of members of British labor unions. In addition, he advocated the setting up of a United States of Europe, which, he said, by including about half the skilled workers of the then-industrialized world under a socialist government, would spread socialist policies throughout the rest of the world by example.

Orwell's anti-communism also appeared early. During the 1930s he admitted only suspicions, pointing out how difficult it was to discover the truth about what was going on in Soviet Russia. For example, he pointed out that evidence and statistics suggested its people were simultaneously the hungriest and the best fed, the most advanced and the most backward, the happiest and the most miserable people in the world. By 1941, however, when many others were praising the cleverness of Stalin's foreign policy in its wavering between alliance and enmity toward Germany, he said the policy would eventually be recognized as opportunistic and stupid. When *Animal Farm* appeared in 1945 (it was written in 1943), Orwell had no intention of deceiving anyone with its allegory. And, by 1948, he wrote openly, in *The Observer*, of the communist experiment as a lost revolution:

> Placed as they were, the Russian Communists necessarily developed into a permanent ruling caste . . . recruited not by birth but by adoption. Since they could not risk the growth of opposition, and since they silenced criticism, they often made avoidable mistakes; then, because they could not admit that their mistakes were their own, they had to find scapegoats, sometimes on an enormous scale.

In short, throughout his adult life and work, George Orwell remained a fiercely honest man, even with himself. Though he well understood the dangers of socialism, he remained committed to the socialist solution to the political and social problems of the world. He believed that if people understood the dangers, they could avoid them. He knew that socialism meant organization of industry as well as of people, which meant the necessity for further growth of the machine-dependent civilization that he had criticized in *The Road to Wigan Pier* and in *Coming Up for Air*, and that this meant the further destruction of the old country way of life which he loved. He was, however, willing to sacrifice even this if all men could be guaranteed a decent standard of living. He was emphatic that improving man's physical conditions would not solve all man's problems: he believed that the most serious of these problems were not physical but rather spiritual and psychological. But he believed that these more serious problems could not be dealt with until man had conquered his material difficulties — through socialism.

The chief theoretical conflict for Orwell was caused by his awareness of individual human differences, which interfere with the abstract group philosophy of socialism. He was himself a sincere and courageous individualist, and he feared the loss of individual freedom that he knew socialism involved. He was honest enough, despite this awareness, to admit that he saw no answer other than socialism to the world's horrible material problems.

Orwell is often praised for his contribution to making people aware of the dangers of communism. Yet his greatest contribution may turn out to be the lesson he taught about the importance of the individual, so easily threatened by *any* form of dictatorship. This lesson he taught not only by his writings, but by the example of his own person: proud, honest, free, and compassionate — no matter what his economic and political beliefs.

Introduction to *Animal Farm*

In 1947 George Orwell said, "*Animal Farm* was the first book in which I tried, with full consciousness of what I was doing, to fuse political purpose and artistic purpose into one whole." He also stated, "The opinion that art should have nothing to do with politics is itself a political attitude. . . . Every line of serious work that I have written since 1936 has been written, directly or indirectly, *against* totalitarianism and *for* democratic socialism, as I understand it . . . it is invariably where I lacked a *political* purpose that I wrote lifeless books. . . ."

These statements from his essay "Why I Write" give us a clear picture of Orwell's motivations. His preoccupation with politics and the state of the world is the key to understanding his intent. He claimed there was no such thing as a neutral book, that every writer displayed a "tendency," and in his own work, he tried frankly to make an art form of political writing with intent to persuade. He wrote propaganda in its true sense (that is, taking sides but not necessarily telling lies, as the modern uses of propaganda might lead us to believe). For Orwell, the "art for art's sake" credo of many writers seemed a sterile and useless proposition.

Thus, *Animal Farm*, the first book to bring him widespread fame, proclaims its political message unashamedly. *Animal Farm* is a little book, but a full one; it is short of volume, long on mass, to borrow some terminology from physics. It is astonishing how clearly Orwell has distilled the essence of his life's thought and work into this superficially simple little story. Its source lies in the chapters of political analysis of the Spanish War in his earlier (and much lesser) realistic novel, *Homage to Catalonia*, and the grim and cheerless world of *1984* is implicit in the pig-bossed conclusion of *Animal Farm*.

The book was written in 1943 and 1944, toward the end of World War II, at a time when criticism of Russia was not an overly popular practice in England, when the Western Allies still had hopes of living in peace with Russia. But Orwell had learned things earlier about communism that we take for granted today. He knew that a Stalin in power offered little more hope for the ideal of the classless society than any other overlord; he believed firmly with Lord Acton that "absolute power corrupts absolutely."

In 1945, the unpopularity of the theme was such that four publishers rejected *Animal Farm*. It might never have seen print at all had it not been such a good-humored jibe on the surface, a whimsical animal story in itself. The necessity of coloring an attack on Russia in this way turned out to be a fortunate thing after all. According to the noted critic, Laurence Brander, *Animal Farm* is Orwell's "most effective sermon; many preachers are most successful with adults during the children's sermon." And by sheer good chance publication came in the summer of 1945. It arrived in the bookstores at the moment when Russia's true methods of establishing control were disillusioning the hopeful world. *Animal Farm* took the reading public by storm; it was soon translated into all the major languages and sold well in them all. Even communists enjoy it, apparently appreciating some of the levels it can be read on while ignoring the one that applies to them.

Animal Farm is a multilevel book. First, and most obviously, it is a wryly humorous animal story. Next, it is a pointed attack on Stalinism, satirizing the events of the Russian Revolution and the rise of Russian Communism. More deeply still, it is a wistful lament for the fate of revolutions in general and a diagram of the ways in which power corrupts.

Orwell believed in revolutions — or wanted to — if they were meant to achieve the classless society and the decency which he idealized. His own experience of revolution in Spain, however, plus what was happening in Russia and his observations of life, forced pessimism upon him. He came to feel that unless men were very, very careful, all revolutions were doomed to meet the fate of the animals' revolt, that far from achieving more than a fleeting equality ("all animals are equal . . ."), the mass of humanity would actually find that they had only changed tyrants, and there would be little to choose between the old and new (". . . but some animals are more equal than others"). Revolutionary fervor is doomed to be overwhelmed by the lust for power of those sufficiently smart and sufficiently unscrupulous to seize it. This pessimism had engulfed Orwell by the time he wrote *1984*; in *Animal Farm* the humor of the story makes it more palatable — and, therefore, quite possibly more effective.

A classic is a book that survives the test of time. Will *Animal Farm* become a classic? It seems to be well on its way to doing so. A good animal story has nine lives, and the book may become a perennial for young people, as good satires often do after their significance on other levels has become too dated or forgotten by all but scholars. (We have only to think of *Gulliver's Travels*, *Alice in Wonderland*, many of H.G. Wells' books, even certain nursery rhymes.)

But *Animal Farm* seems likely to survive as a serious work, too. The parable is a time-honored form, and in the hands of a master storyteller, its teaching potential and memorability are great. It probably will not matter if the anti-communist satire of *Animal Farm* remains intelligible. Already the specifics of its protest against Stalinism require considerable explanation for the younger generation, but its satire on corrupted revolution and the misuse of power remains completely clear. Given human nature, it will unfortunately remain clear as long as society resembles anything in the world today.

Background, Political and Historical

On one important level, *Animal Farm* is a satire on the history of Russia under Communist rule, from the Revolution in 1917 to the Teheran Conference in 1943. To fully appreciate the satire, it is important to have an understanding of the Revolution itself, as well as the events and people that caused it.

Marxism

The Russian Revolution was partly the inspiration of Karl Marx, a German economist and the founder of revolutionary communism. With Friedrich Engels, he elaborated his theories in the famous *Communist Manifesto* (1848) and *Das Kapital* (1867-94).

The main tenet of Marxist theory is that *economic* relations are the most important relations between people. It then teaches that in making any finished product, there are several elements: raw materials, factory and machinery, the factory manager and owner (called the capitalist), and the workman. Of all of these elements, Marx says, the workman is the most important, for it is he who transforms the raw material into the finished product and thus makes it more valuable. Yet it is the capitalist who takes the extra value as his ''profit.'' Marx further states that though such capitalism may once have been necessary in creating the modern world, it is no longer necessary and, in fact, *causes* the suffering of the workmen who make up the largest number of people in society.

Marx's solution is for the workmen to take over from the capitalists the other elements (''means'') of production: raw materials, factories, homes, and so on. Communist theory here departs from socialism (in which Orwell believed). Socialism considers that the way to take over the means of production is legally and constitutionally (for example, by the British Labour Party policy of purchasing industries). Marxist Communism, however, considers that *only* by violent revolution can common men take over the means of production from the capitalists.

According to Marx, private property, as such, is an evil. His reason is his belief that even after a revolution, in which the common men have gained control, the more clever men would eventually reclaim the means of production and become the new capitalists. To prevent this, he says, private property must be abolished. All the people must own all the property collectively; no man should individually own anything except the barest personal necessities. Socialism, on the other hand, makes a distinction between the means of production and consumer goods (those products we use or consume). According to socialist theory, the means of production, once legally obtained, should be collectively owned, but consumer goods, including what we would consider as private property, should be owned by individuals.

Marx was an idealist, dreaming of a paradise on earth in which all men were free and equal, and enjoyed a good standard of living. The necessary stages in progress to this paradise are, first, the violent revolution, and then the "dictatorship of the common men" (by which Marx meant that after the revolution, those men who were members of the Communist Party should assume complete leadership). Eventually, said Marx, this dictatorship would "wither away," and all men would be free and equal. Marx never explained *how* this process of "withering" would come about.

The Communist Revolution

Marxism and other socialist theories were advocated by various groups in Russia at the end of the nineteenth century and in the early years of this century when the despotic Russian monarchy still kept the common people in cruel, medieval serfdom, amounting to slavery. Although there was great wealth in the country, it was not industrialized to the extent of Western Europe. Most of the people were illiterate, and very miserable living conditions were common. There was, however, an educated middle class and it was with them that the theories of reform and revolution began.

In 1914, Russia entered World War I on the side of the Allies against Germany. Russia was badly weakened by the war and the government lost its foothold. The people revolted, under the leadership of various revolutionary associations, and the revolution that Marx had predicted was accomplished in 1917. The Tsar was deposed (and eventually executed) and the bureaucratic government toppled.

At first, the Mensheviks, a socialist revolutionary party, took over the government, but it had many rivals. Of the Russian revolutionary parties, the Bolsheviks, led by Lenin, were the strongest, and in 1918 they took power by force. Lenin established the "dictatorship of the common man" — of the Bolshevik party.

Civil war continued for some time, and Great Britain, France and the U.S. sent troops to Russia to help restore the monarchy. For a number of reasons they soon withdrew. Meanwhile, the Bolsheviks struck, seized control, and consolidated the government against internal and external enemies.

Lenin was a strict Marxist in theory but, during the time that he led Soviet Russia (especially after 1921), he compromised in practice. He allowed some private enterprise as an incentive, even importing American engineers and businessmen so as to adopt American methods and advance the backward (even feudal) Russian economy. Ford had by this time shown the value of his mass-production methods, and he became the Soviet ideal. When Lenin died in 1924 (from overwork, it is said), he had become a hero of godlike proportions. His body was preserved in state, on view in the Lenin Mausoleum in Moscow (originally part of the Royal Palace).

Stalin as Leader

When Lenin died, there was a struggle for power among his chief lieutenants, especially Trotsky and Stalin. Trotsky advocated world revolution, while Stalin opposed this policy, wanting to concentrate on developing Russia's strength. Stalin eventually won the battle for power, and Trotsky was reduced in position, sent to the further reaches of Russia, and finally, in 1927, exiled. He was harassed wherever he went and was accused several times of being the principal plotter against the Stalinist regime. The last accusations came during the treason trials of the 1930s, and he was sentenced, in his absence, to death. He was finally assassinated in Mexico in 1940.

After Trotsky's expulsion, Stalin entrenched himself in power with the help of an effective propaganda system, including control of all information outlets such as newspapers, and of the secret police (the Cheka or OGPU). Between 1927 and 1932 he eliminated such competitors as Rykov, Bukharin, and Kamenov. He reversed Lenin's policy of allowing a certain amount of private enterprise and replaced it with more socialization and successive five-year plans — plans for the economic improvement of the country. The first five-year plan (originally suggested by Trotsky), begun in 1928, was an attempt to industrialize Russia on a grand scale. Stalin at the same time tried to nationalize agriculture. He seized the farmlands and organized collectives of peasants to farm them; he exiled the farmer-owners of the land (the mujiks), who suffered enormous hardships. These hardships were shared in a very short time by the majority of Russian people, for Stalin's methods crippled agriculture and famine swept the country. About five million peasants died.

Because of these bad results, in his second five-year plan Stalin gave more scope for individual effort and initiative — and more reward. At the same time, during the 1934 purges, he pressed millions of men into forced labor, on the excuse that they would not conform to his laws. Another purge in 1936-37 (while the Spanish Civil War was going on) eliminated many of the top Party men whom Stalin felt were a threat to his power. He emerged as an almost godlike figure-leader, encouraging the worship of his followers.

Stalin and Nazi Germany

One of the main planks of Stalin's policy in the 1930s was opposition to German Nazism, especially since the Nazis were anti-communist, and imprisoned German communists. Each power described the other in its propaganda as agents of the devil. The two countries were the main powers behind the scenes in the Spanish Civil War, the Germans aiding Franco, Russia being on the side of government. As late as March, 1939, Stalin denounced Hitler as an aggressor, yet in August of that same year, while he was actually negotiating a mutual alliance with Britain and France, Stalin suddenly announced the signing of a nonagression pact with Germany. Russia in this way acquired eastern Poland and several of the other small Eastern European countries that are behind the Iron Curtain today. Germany took western Poland unopposed. Soviet Russia had changed under Stalin from a Communist country to an imperialistic dictatorship. Stalin's sudden switch of attitude toward Germany was a great shock to those anti-fascists who had been sympathetic to Russian Communism.

When Germany invaded Poland in September, 1939, secured against Russian intervention by the Hitler-Stalin nonagression pact, it was the signal for the start of the World War II. (The world had been torn by military adventures by Japan in China, by Italy in Africa, and by Germany in Europe, since 1931.) The Spanish Civil War was a dress rehearsal for world war since Germany and Italy sent troops, tanks and planes to aid Franco, as well as to try out new methods of war. Germany was swallowing all of Europe; England and France finally issued an ultimatum to Hitler, saying that if he attacked Poland, they would go to war with him. When Hitler and Stalin divided Poland, Britain and France declared war on Germany.

There was a lull in the fighting from the start of war in September, 1939 until April, 1940, when Germany launched a gigantic offensive. Nazi troops occupied Denmark, Norway, Holland, and Belgium, invaded and defeated France, and pushed the British army stationed in France back to the Atlantic coast; the men managed to escape only by boat during the famous evacuation of Dunkirk. The Germans also occupied parts of Greece and North Africa and prepared for what was feared to be an invasion of Britain.

On June 22, 1941, there was another sudden shift in the alignment of the forces in the war. Germany suddenly turned on her ally of less than two years and, in contravention of the Stalin-Hitler pact, German troops invaded Russia. A colossal struggle then began, Germany pressing for as quick a victory as possible, while Russia mobilized the whole country to repel the invader. The struggle seesawed across Russia for two years, at enormous cost in men and materials to both sides, neither side winning a decisive victory.

Having been attacked by Fascist Germany, Communist Russia was accepted for the first time since the Revolution as an ally by the Western Powers (Britain, United States, and France), who aided her with large quantities of war materials. In December, 1943, Britain, United States and Russia met together at Teheran to plan the future strategy of the war. The turning point of the war in Russia came with the Allied invasion of Europe in June, 1944, when Germany had to withdraw troops and material from the Russian front in order to defend herself in the west. This temporary harmony between Russia and the West lasted until, between them, they brought Germany to surrender in May, 1945.

Plot Summary

Just before his death, Old Major, the prize boar of Manor Farm, tells the other animals of his dream of a new life for them and encourages rebellion against the cruel drunkard, Farmer Jones. When an opportunity arises, the animals drive Jones and his men from the farm, rename it Animal Farm, and take over its operation. Almost all participate enthusiastically in the work; the pigs, the cleverest of the animals, assume the administration. They write on the wall of the barn the Seven Commandments of Animalism (their elaboration of Major's ideas), which forbid animals to associate with human beings or to adopt human habits.

Although the boars, Napoleon and Snowball, compete for leadership of the farm, they work together to beat off Jones when he attempts to recapture the farm. Snowball shows special bravery in this Battle of the Cowshed. Afterwards, the rivalry between the two deepens, focussing finally on Snowball's idea for bringing the animals a better life by building a windmill. Napoleon opposes the idea and has his rival chased from the farm by his bodyguard of dogs. He takes over the project of the windmill as his own.

With the work on the windmill and the increasing appetites of the nonproductive pigs and dogs, the living conditions of the other animals worsen. At every opportunity, the banished Snowball is used as a scapegoat by Napoleon. The Commandments are transformed one by one to justify the pigs' actions as they sell produce to human beings and adopt human comforts. Whenever the animals question anything, the threat of Jones' return is used to silence them.

When the windmill, only partly completed, collapses in a storm, the pigs blame Snowball again and announce an all-winter project to rebuild it. To suppress increasing dissatisfaction, Napoleon purges the farm of malcontents: several pigs and other animals. All confess to being agents of Snowball and are executed.

Napoleon becomes an almost legendary, godlike figure: he is called "Leader" and appears only on rare occasions. He institutes negotiations with neighboring human farmers for the sale of some timber. Napoleon appears to discredit Frederick and favor Pilkington, then sells the timber to the former. In the attack that Frederick subsequently makes on the farm, his men blow up the completed windmill.

Although the windmill is rebuilt and prosperity comes to the farm, only the pigs benefit, and they grow more like humans all the time. One day they appear walking on their hind legs and carrying whips. And only one altered Commandment remains: "All animals are equal, but some animals are more equal than others."

From outside the farmhouse, the working animals observe Napoleon entertaining his human neighbors. It is impossible any longer to distinguish the pigs from the men.

Characters in the Novel

OLD MAJOR: The venerable old boar whose vision of a better life and call for rebellion are the inspiration for the founding of Animal Farm.

SNOWBALL: A young boar whose persuasive speech, organizational ability and intelligent plans make him a contender for the leadership of Animal Farm.

NAPOLEON: Another young boar whose ambition and direct approach to gaining power cause him to win the struggle for leadership of Animal Farm.

BOXER: A cart horse of immense strength, great loyalty, and small intelligence, who is foremost in projects requiring physical labor.

CLOVER: A mare whose motherly concern for Boxer and the other animals makes her a source of personal strength for all, especially during difficult times.

BENJAMIN: A donkey whose skepticism about social change and human nature persists unchanged.

MOSES: A raven who regales the animals with stories about the better life to come on Sugarcandy Mountain.

MOLLIE: A mare whose frivolous attitude and vanity eventually cause her to leave Animal Farm and go to work for the owner of a tavern.

SQUEALER: A fast-talking porker who is used by Napoleon as chief henchman and propagandist.

JONES: The human owner of Manor Farm who is driven from his property by the animals.

FREDERICK AND PILKINGTON: Neighboring farmers.

THE DOGS: A group of fierce hounds, trained by Napoleon from puppyhood to serve as his bodyguards and secret police; three are named Bluebell, Jessie, and Pincher.

THE CAT: An individualist who votes with both sides of any question but supports neither.

THE SHEEP: The uneducated masses who can (or will) grasp only oversimplified principles, but whom Napoleon finds useful for bleating slogans.

MR. WHYMPER: A sly human attorney, hired as an agent or middleman for transactions between Animal Farm and humans.

MURIEL: A white goat who has learned to read quite well.

Chapter Summaries and Commentaries

CHAPTER 1

Old Major's Dream

Summary

After Mr. Jones, the drunken owner of Manor Farm, has staggered up to bed, Old Major, the aged and respected prize boar, leads a meeting attended by all the animals on the Farm. Major describes the lives, "miserable, laborious and short," of the animals. The land itself, he insists, could support them. The cause of their misery is man's greed. Man steals what the animals produce, and as soon as an individual animal's usefulness comes to an end, he is cruelly slaughtered.

Man is animalkind's only enemy, says Major. If they expelled man, they would gain their freedom and comfort. He urges the animals to revolt but adds that they should not adopt man's evil habits when they are free: they should have nothing at all to do with man. He states that all animals are equal and concludes by telling them of a dream he had had of a song, called "Beasts of England," which describes the ideal society of the future. The animals are excited by the vision and learn this song, which so pleases them that they sing it over and over again, until they awake Mr. Jones. The meeting hurriedly ends as the farmer turns his shotgun on the barn wall, where he believes a fox to be attacking his animals.

Commentary

Much of the direct impact of the novel depends upon Orwell's management of point of view. This chapter immediately establishes that the story is told impersonally but through the eyes of the animals who make up the body of "average citizens" of Animal Farm. This choice of point of view has several consequences. It keeps the human beings in the background as far as possible. It encourages the reader to believe, for the purposes of the story, that the animals do act as they are shown to. It eventually makes it possible for Orwell to show the good will and hopes of the ordinary animals slowly undermined and destroyed by the selfish machinations of the pigs. In short, it is exactly the right point of view from which to present the novel most effectively.

Just as the point of view is established no later than the second paragraph of the novel, so also are the characters quickly drawn for the reader. They are, of course, not fully developed personalities but easily recognized character types. The animals have an interesting combination of traits: just animal enough, just human enough, to be believable. Roughly, their actions are characteristic of animals; their ideas and words, of human beings. Were Orwell to have forgotten this combination, what happens would not have the plausibility it does. The way Boxer and Clover walk into the barn among the other animals and the way the cat looks after her own comfort are but two instances in this chapter of the book's faithfulness to animal behavior. Obviously, Old Major's speech in the barn is a signal that the reader is to expect the animals to talk and think like human beings. (Orwell, by the way, is careful never to admit the reader to the mind of any of the animals.)

Orwell's careful, rapid establishing of point of view and characters allows him to establish immediately a situation in which the reader is sympathetic to the animals but knows they are doomed to failure.

It is the reader's awareness of human nature that allows Orwell to suggest in a single, short chapter so ironical a situation. He quite safely assumes the reader knows that most ironical fact: the good idea can easily become the evil idea. Irony goes hand in hand with satire, and nothing is more ironical than Old Major's well-intentioned speech before he dies. The revered leader is giving his final wisdom to the animals, and the vision he depicts of a better life is persuasive and ought to be true. But in his words, as the reader can see, lies the possibility for just the opposite of the good life he speaks of.

Unfortunately for the animals, it is out of this speech that the entire idea of Animal Farm comes, as well as the principles on which it is to be operated. Old Major's view of life is simple: man is bad; animals are good. His vision for the future of the animals is also simple; it is nostalgic and pastoral, as shown in the song "Beasts of England." Both are, as the reader quickly sees, oversimplified. They are the strength of Animal Farm in the beginning, but they will become its major weakness as time goes on. For the purposes of Orwell's satire, everything grows out of the speech.

On the level of plot, everything that happens comes from the speech, too. Expecting the rebellion to come in some indefinable time in the future, the animals are not prepared for having the freedom Old Major envisions. They are easily led by whoever is ambitious enough to assume leadership. And they are likewise easily led to believe that everything that occurs is done in their behalf, although soon this is not so. Old Major's vision has such a lasting effect that finally the animals will act against their own welfare. They will realize only too late that they have been duped, as of course they had always been, in a sense, by human beings.

The structure of the novel is a slow rise, then a slow fall. It might be described as a circle, except that the animals will not really be back to the point at which they started by the end of the story. Whereas under Jones they are victims, by the end of the story they are unwittingly the cause of their own undoing.

In this first chapter, though, it is important to see that Orwell has established a situation in which Major's protest is absolutely justified. In the first place, from the animals' viewpoint at least, there is a valid objection to giving all their labor and their very bodies entirely to the needs and pleasures of man. Moreover, Farmer Jones is revealed as an incompetent, irresponsible owner who cares more for a drink than for an orderly farm.

His obvious negligence is an encouragement to the revolt of the animals.

Glossary

"Beasts of England"—Several commentators point out the parody on the "Internationale," the anthem of international Communism: "Arise, ye prisoners of starvation!/Arise, ye slaves, no more in thrall. . . ."

Boar—a pig used for breeding.

Dissentients—those who disagree with the majority opinion.

Eighteen hands high—six feet high, to the shoulder (a "hand" is four inches).

Knacker—a person who buys old animals (often horses) to slaughter them and use the carcasses for pet food and other commercial purposes.

La Cucaracha—a Mexican folksong, associated with the Mexican struggle for independence.

Mangel-Wurzels (Mangels)—large beets used as cattle food.

Middle White—a breed of pig, chiefly used for pork.

News of the World—a popular British weekly newspaper, known for its sensational coverage of crimes and other events.

"Our lives are miserable, laborious and short"—an echo of the pessimistic philosopher Thomas Hobbes, who wrote, in 1651, that the life of the peasant was "solitary, poor, nasty, brutish, and short."

Paddock—small field, enclosure for horses.

Pop-holes—small holes serving hens as exits from the hen house.

Scullery—back kitchen.

"The produce of our labor. . ."—a clear reference to a key concept in the thought of Marx: who is entitled to what is produced by laborers?

Trap—small, horse-drawn carriage.

Tushes—tusks; pointed canine teeth.

CHAPTER 2

The Rebellion

Summary

Old Major dies soon after the meeting. He has inspired the animals to prepare for rebellion and, for three months, there is much excited, secret discussion. The pigs are the cleverest of the animals and, led by Snowball, Napoleon and Squealer, they elaborate Major's ideas into a system called Animalism, which they teach to the other animals. At first the animals make stupid objections that the pigs find difficult to answer. In addition, the pigs must compete with the delicious promises of Moses the Raven about a world in the sky, Sugarcandy Mountain, to which animals go when they die. The pigs work hard to convince the other animals, and regular meetings are held in the barn.

In the meantime, Jones' management of the farm becomes worse and worse, until one day he neglects to feed the animals. When the animals break into the storehouse and begin to feed themselves, Jones and his men start to beat them and drive them back. It is this crisis that brings about the animals' actual rebellion; it is unexpected and unplanned. Once their hunger leads them to behave so extraordinarily, they rise up against their master spontaneously and chase all humans from the farm. Moses the Raven follows the humans.

The animals then proceed to destroy all traces of man's rule: bits and traces, collars, knives, blinkers and especially the whips. Visiting the farmhouse in awe, they decide that no animal should ever live in it. The pigs, who have already learned to read and write, change the name of Manor Farm to Animal Farm. They also write on the wall of the barn the Seven Commandments that have been elaborated from Major's ideas. The Commandments, which are to serve as the "unalterable" law of Animal Farm, distinguish animals from humans, forbid animals to wear clothes, sleep in a bed, or drink alcohol, and state that all animals are equal.

It is harvest time, and Snowball convinces the animals to join together and get the harvest in. They go off to do so, but not before Napoleon has taken away the cows' milk for himself and the other pigs.

Commentary

The differences among the animals that make possible the direction the plot takes are vividly shown in this chapter, as elsewhere. Obviously, Snowball and Napoleon will be the leaders of Animal Farm; even before the Rebellion they set to work planning for the time when it will occur. Their natural abilities are such that the other animals go along with them without thinking about what they are doing. But the different temperaments and views of life of Snowball and Napoleon — shown, for example, in the way Snowball patiently corrects Mollie's self-centered ideas during the discussion of Animalism and the way Napoleon handles the disposition of the milk — predict a rivalry between the two for which, as it turns out, the other animals suffer.

Boxer and Clover are the unintelligent but faithful party rank and file and, although they may grumble and doubt in times to come, they have the virtue of unswerving loyalty. In between these two and the two chief pigs range all the other animals: from Squealer, who will be used by Napoleon, to Benjamin, the perpetual skeptic.

It is ironical that from the start the animals accept the pigs so readily as their leaders. The pigs are never said to be better than the other animals; they are only smarter or more clever. The value of intelligence, in a social sense, at least, depends on why is it used, the motives of those who have it.

The scene of the Rebellion is as ironical as other things in the story. The animals do not intend to start a rebellion; they are only hungry because of the neglect of Jones and his men. Orwell presents the Rebellion in just two paragraphs, partly to emphasize the accidental way in which the new society starts. (This lack of detail also contrasts sharply with the way he treats later importent scenes: for example, the Battle of the Cowshed or the Battle of the Windmill.) The scene is also one in which the reader is intended to ask "but what if the animals had been fed in time?" or some other quite practical question. Historical necessity, to use the appropriate Marxist term, is really historical accident in Orwell's eyes.

What has been only a dream and a hope for Old Major quickly becomes a system called Animalism, drawn up exclusively by Snowball, Napoleon, and Squealer. On one level of Orwell's satire, it is, of course, parallel with Marxism, but it could be any set of idealistic principles, especially any set that is not carefully worked out, that pays too much attention to immediate and obvious grievances, too little to basic problems and individual needs.

Even the name given to the set of doctrines, later embodied in the Seven Commandments, is itself revealing. Orwell's sure, critical sense of propaganda is apparent here. It is a name designed to arouse "national" pride, to encourage a sense of exclusiveness. It is also a name that reveals an essential fact about Animal Farm: it is based on a fear of man as the ever-present enemy. Several times in the novel, all Squealer will have to do in order to bend the animals to some impossible task is to ask if they want Jones back as their master. Animalism is clearly propaganda, not a workable system.

It is important to read the Seven Commandments closely for the outcome of the novel and the revolt hinges on whether they are kept or not. Note, too, their irony. All except the last are based upon the belief that man is evil. When the threat of man has been removed, it is possible that someone with selfish aims can pervert both the spirit and the letter of these commandments. What is taken, in good faith, in one way can become something else — as the story demonstrates.

The first truly ominous note is struck at the end of the chapter.

Napoleon says the milk should be left but, when the animals return from the fields, it is missing.

Also worth noting in this chapter are the characters of Mollie and Moses. Mollie, the white mare, is solely concerned with her own comfort and appearance; she is vanity itself and cares not a whit for the Rebellion. Moses, the raven, speaks always of Sugarcandy Mountain, which is a kind of jocular parallel of the theological heaven. He is an adversary of the movement because he is preaching something over and beyond Animalism, and when Mr. Jones is chased away Moses follows after him. Both are familiar character types in the "real" world of humanity, and every attempt at reform or revolution encounters them.

Glossary

Berkshire—a breed of pig, often used for ham.

Carpet bag—luggage made of carpeting material.

Linseed cake—the solid cake left after the oil is pressed from flax seed; used as animal food.

Lithograph—picture printed in ink from a master plate.

Porker—pig raised for food (compare "boar," Chapter 1).

Queen Victoria—Queen of Great Britain from 1837 to 1901; she was very popular.

Spinney—a small woods or clump of trees.

Trotters—pigs' front hoofs.

Windsor chair—a simple chair made entirely of wood with a curved back-support.

CHAPTER 3

The Pigs Take Over

Summary

The harvest, a bumper crop, is taken in in record time. The awkwardness of the animals in using human implements is offset by their greater knowledge of the work and the fields, by their enthusiasm, and by the fact that, unlike human farm laborers, no animal steals anything for himself. The pigs organize and lead the others, doing no physical work themselves. Boxer works especially heroically, and it is as much through his efforts as the pigs' cleverness that the harvest is a success.

During the rest of the summer the animals work happily, their daily lives organized by the pigs. Sunday is the day of rest. The new flag of Animal Farm (an old green tablecloth with a white hoof and horn painted on it) is raised every Sunday morning, after which the animals' meeting takes place. The next week's work is planned out at this meeting.

Snowball and Napoleon, the leaders, can never agree. Snowball organizes the Sunday afternoon recreation time, setting up various animal committees, the most successful of which is the reading and writing class. Napoleon, on the other hand, concentrates on educating the young, taking a litter of puppies away from their mother and secluding them in a loft. Over the protests of the other animals, the pigs reserve for themselves not only all the milk but the apple crop as well, explaining that these are necessary for the pigs' ''brain work.'' Their most convincing argument is that if they fail in their work, Jones will come back.

Commentary

In the early days of the new order Orwell shows the lot of the animals as considerably improved. The animals are obviously inspired, and they work and live accordingly. Only Mollie and Benjamin are discontent and for quite different reasons. Mollie, as we have seen, is deplorably vain and self-obsessed; all that matters to her is her own comfort. Benjamin, however, is unmoved by the revolution because of his wise caution; he has lived too long and seen too much to be swept away by a tide of enthusiasm. He watches and waits, skeptical of the outcome.

On the surface, at first, his caution seems too great. Under the particular urging of Snowball, the society of Animal Farm quickly begins to take on all the characteristics of ''civilized'' human society: meetings, committees, and the like. Yet it is through such ''democratic'' events that Orwell foreshadows much of what is to come. For instance, at meetings only Snowball and Napoleon introduce resolutions; the other animals can think of nothing to propose. Before long they will simply be taking orders, as if from Jones, not even voting. Snowball and Napoleon disagree, as their different temperaments lead the reader to expect them to. A real struggle for power is beginning here, and it is only a matter of time before one deposes the other. Who will win this struggle is clear enough from the hints Orwell has dropped so far.

The animals are unable to manage committee organization but, to a greater or lesser extent, learn to read and write. They are the masses, ready to vote but unable to understand what they are voting for or against. What moves them most is the threat of Jones' return. The disposition of the milk earlier, and now the apples, foreshadows the increasing privileges the pigs take, in every way making themselves into the ruling class. Even Napoleon's taking the puppies under his personal care is ominous. It may not at first be apparent why he wants to raise them himself, but the adjective "sturdy" for the puppies gives us some clue, as does the seclusion and secrecy with which he operates.

What is being shown here, in Orwell's satire, is the struggle for power that occurs after the death or fall of a great, visionary leader. More generally, it is the struggle that occurs in any society in which the people at large really have no voice. This is shown, in one form, in Snowball's simplification of the seven Commandments into one slogan: "Four legs good, two legs bad." The sheep are especially satisfied with this reduction of doctrine and are given to chanting it. It is just the kind of slogan that is easy to understand, dangerously simple, and flexible enough to manipulate for those bent on holding power.

At the end of the chapter, the structure of the novel is still in the rising stage, but everywhere are the elements by which the falling stage will inevitably be reached. The reader realizes the fall cannot really begin, much less accelerate, until Napoleon has gotten rid of Snowball, an idealist who genuinely has the good of all animals as his aim for leadership. Once that is accomplished, the second half of the structure will be under way.

That end is implicit in the events of this chapter. Orwell seems to imply that the revolution might have a chance of success if Snowball were able to have his way; he truly attempts to educate the other animals to the point of making decisions for themselves. On the other hand, he cannot prevent Napoleon's rise and he does nothing to contradict Squealer, who is emerging as the tricky propagandist of the privileged class. And there is no question that the pigs are making themselves a privileged class, in spite of the seventh commandment, which says that all animals are equal. Their keeping the apples all for themselves is the first significant violation of the Animalist creed. What the animals had fought for is now being taken from them by their own kind — a reversal all too common in the history of human revolutions.

Glossary

Cutter—a horse-drawn farm implement, used for mowing.

Flag with hoof and horn—the symbolism is comparable to that of the Soviet flag with its hammer and sickle, which represents the industrial proletariat and the rural peasants united.

Horse-rake—a horse-drawn farm implement, used for raking.

Tread it out—separate the grain from the straw and chaff.

Animal committees—probably in part a reference to the many well-disciplined "Workers' Committees" organized by Trotsky immediately after the Soviet Revolution. Their purpose was to educate the illiterate masses, both generally and in the principles of Marxism.

CHAPTER 4

The Battle of the Cowshed

Summary

Pigeons are sent by Napoleon and Snowball to teach the neighboring animals about Animalism and to tell them about the Rebellion. At first the neighboring farmers paid little attention to Jones' loss, but now they become frightened as their own farm animals grow disobedient. Mr. Pilkington of Foxwood Farm and Mr. Frederick of Pinchfield Farm, the nearest neighbors, spread false rumors about the "terrible wickedness" of the animals on Animal Farm.

Eventually, Jones and his men, with the help of his neighbors, attack Animal Farm. The animals have prepared a careful defence against attack. In an excellent display of military tactics, Snowball leads the attackers into ambush. Boxer strikes down a stableboy, and the frightened men are chased once more from the Farm. Boxer's sorrow for the boy is unnecessary, for the lad soon runs off. The animals hold a victory celebration and confer medals on Snowball and Boxer. The battle is named the Battle of the Cowshed, and its memory is to be celebrated every year.

Commentary

Toward the beginning of this chapter, propaganda is used openly by both sides: by Animal Farm, at the instigation of Snowball and Napoleon, to try to persuade animals on other farms to join with them in the spirit of rebellion against the tyranny of their masters; by the owners of the neighboring farms of Foxwood and Pinchfield, to try to discredit the new society of Animal Farm by circulating rumors of excesses in the animals' behavior and failures in their attempts to govern themselves.

The general satirical point of the chapter is that the Rebellion is helped by the incompetence, quarrelling, and greed of its opponents. Foxwood and Pinchfield obviously care more about what they can get from the situation than about what they can do to help Jones reclaim his property. Only when they begin to fear a loss of law and order (or worse) from their own animals do they take any action. Moreover, the attempt to retake the farm might have succeeded if the men had planned together more or had not been so easily divided and frightened off by the dedicated revolutionaries.

The idea will recur toward the end of the book when the humans re-enter the picture. One of Orwell's constant targets of criticism is the tendency of both nations and individuals to use the troubles of others as opportunities to improve their own positions, rather than work together in a genuine spirit of co-operation.

In contrast, the animals' strategy is well planned in advance by Snowball, and the animals perform like a disciplined army, heedless of their personal safety. They are still in a stage in which they feel a sense of their own existence in a community, and their pride in winning the battle serves to deepen their commitment to the Rebellion.

In plot detail, the battle serves another purpose. Later in the story, when Snowball has been driven from Animal Farm by Napoleon, the latter will use the events of the Battle of the Cowshed to accuse his adversary of deception and cowardice. Snowball's actions in the battle are such that they can be described in unflattering terms by Napoleon later, although now Snowball is acclaimed a hero and is decorated.

This is one reason the Battle of the Cowshed is described in so much greater detail than that of the Rebellion. Orwell's main use of the scene is, however, satire through what is called a *mock epic*. In this literary device a great battle or war is reduced to the barnyard level. The irony is great because matters of immediate life and death are described in such everyday, apparently unimportant terms.

The irony of the Battle of the Cowshed is not restricted to that of the mock epic. The reader also realizes the irony of the animals defending, at the risk of losing their own lives, a society in which power has never been theirs and never really will be. The irony, in this case, does not lead to humor, as it sometimes does, but rather to an awareness that man often does not know what he does but yet must act. Like most soldiers, the animals go into battle with the best of intentions; only later will they realize that they have been duped. Then it will be too late.

Also worth noting in this chapter are the opportunities Orwell uses to define characters further. Mollie, for example, avoids the battle altogether and goes off into hiding. Boxer, with his great strength and determination, winds up a hero. We also see another side of Boxer, one that was only faintly intimated before: his moral goodness. He is terribly upset when it appears that the boy he kicks is dead.

In fact, there are many such small touches in this chapter. As critics have often pointed out, *Animal Farm* is so effective partly because of the convincing details Orwell includes. Here, for example, is the naming of the battle by the inhabitants of Animal Farm and the giving of decorations and establishing of days to celebrate in the revolutionary calendar. They are the kinds of details that are persuasive because they are exactly the sort of thing that people do in such circumstances.

Glossary

Gentleman farmer—one who owns or even runs a farm but does not depend on it for his living.

Had their females in common—shared their wives. The reference is to the principle of easy divorce, prevalent in Russia for a short time after the Revolution.

Hunters—horses used for hunting, especially fox-hunting.

Julius Caesar's campaigns—Roman statesman and soldier, famous for (among many other things) his tactics in the Gallic wars. His descriptions and commentaries on these are often used as a sort of primer of the Latin language, a subject required for any sort of education in England as late as Orwell's day.

October 12th—the anniversary of the Bolshevik uprising of 1917, the beginning of the Russian revolution.

CHAPTER 5

The Banishment of Snowball

Summary

Vain and empty-headed Mollie is seen to be more interested in sugar and ribbons (marks of human enslavement) than in the new animal society and finally disappears from Animal Farm. She is soon discovered to be pulling a cart for the owner of a tavern.

In January, the farm falls on hard times when the weather becomes too cold to work. The pigs spend their time planning the next season's work; their ideas are presented to many meetings to be discussed and voted upon by the other animals. The rivalry between Napoleon and Snowball interferes. Most of the new schemes are developed by Snowball, while Napoleon seems to be waiting for Snowball to fail. One argument that develops between the two is over combating any future threat from humans: Napoleon suggests plans to improve the defenses of the farm, while Snowball advocates spreading the rebellion to the other farms, to free the whole country.

The breaking point is reached when Snowball proposes building a windmill to produce electric power to heat the farm, run the machinery and, in fact, do much of the animals' work for them. Napoleon, says that the windmill will not work and that they should concentrate on increasing food production. Snowball works very hard on the plans, and the others, excepting cynical Benjamin, take sides. A meeting of the animals is called to debate the idea. Snowball is on the point of convincing the animals to adopt his plan when suddenly Napoleon calls in his bodyguard of nine fierce dogs (they have grown from the puppies raised by Napoleon). The dogs chase Snowball from the platform and off the farm. The other animals are too frightened to say anything, much less take any action.

Napoleon immediately abolishes the democratic discussions of the animals and takes over the management of the farm personally. Squealer explains all of this as necessary to prevent the return of Jones and suggests that Snowball is "no better than a criminal." From this time on, the animals assemble on Sundays only to receive orders, salute the flag, venerate the skull of Major, and sing "Beasts of England." The growling of the dogs prevents any possible protest. Three weeks later Napoleon announces that the windmill is to be built after all. Squealer explains that Napoleon had only seemed to oppose the windmill in order to get rid of Snowball. In fact, says Squealer, it was Napoleon who originally drew up the windmill plans, which were then stolen by Snowball.

Commentary

In the debate over the windmill, the rival leaders act as the reader would expect them to: Snowball is persuasive; Napoleon says little. Only when it looks as if words have won the day does Napoleon summon his dogs and successfully put an end to the threat to power from Snowball.

The speed with which Napoleon takes matters into his own hands shows the care he has taken to prepare for this moment. It is the combination of his planning and the animals' surprise that enables him to seize power with almost no resistance at all. The definite plans he announces and the follow-up propagandizing by Squealer complete the takeover of power.

What has happened, although the animals do not realize this until much later, is the establishment of a dictatorship. The use of a personal bodyguard is one of the first signs. Another is the change of routine: for example, the abolishing of the open meeting every Sunday morning. Yet another is the creation of a (conveniently dead) hero who can be used to give credit to the ruler. Finally, the rival to leadership must be discredited, with fabricated evidence and false arguments that he was an enemy all along.

On one level, Orwell is satirizing the way in which people can be (and often are) deceived when an individual is bent on using them, manipulating them for his own purposes. As in all such instances, what appears to be and what is are quite contradictory things. The disagreements between Snowball and Napoleon, for instance, are but ways by which the latter waits until the right time to attempt his seizure of power. The masses — the animals — know nothing of this and are not even sure they are being used when the moment comes.

Napoleon's takeover of Animal Farm is a clear sign that events are moving to the stage of falling after a rise to a kind of peak. The windmill, for example, was proposed by Snowball as a pinnacle of success for the community of Animal Farm. True, the windmill will be built and rebuilt, but for different reasons. Small details also suggest the way in which events will now move to what they were in the beginning or perhaps worse. A new slogan becomes popular: "Napoleon is always right." The dogs act toward Napoleon as they acted toward Jones or would act toward any human being. Of course, the fact that the animals do not read the foreshadowings of their fate under Napoleon continues to be one of the large ironies of the novel.

Glossary

Basic slag—a by-product of a steel mill, used as fertilizer.

Both in and out of season—at all times, appropriate and otherwise.

Cranks and cog-wheels—shafts and wheels for transmitting power or motion.

Farmer and Stockbreeder—an agricultural magazine.

"File past the skull"—a clear reference to the permanent exhibition in Moscow of the embalmed body of Lenin, who is generally accepted as the father of the Soviet Revolution.

Gaiters—coverings of cloth or leather for the legs, worn on the ankle or below the knee.

Harrows—farm implements, used to break up the soil or drag it to cover seeds.

Incubators—here, an apparatus for hatching chicks by artificial heat.

Public-house—an inn or tavern that provides food and lodging as well as drink.

Publican—keeper of a public-house.

Silage—waste vegetable matter (hay, corn stalk, etc.) put in pits to ferment and be used as winter feed for farm animals.

CHAPTER 6

The Building and Destruction of the Windmill

Summary

In the second year of the new society the animals work even harder; a sixty-hour work week is introduced, as is supposedly volunteer labor on Sunday afternoons (any animal who does not "volunteer" has his food ration cut). Nevertheless, the gigantic task of building the windmill prevents the animals from completing other tasks, and the harvest is less successful than the previous one. Quarrying stone for the windmill's walls proves unexpectedly difficult, and only Boxer's heroic exertions keep the work going.

During this time it is discovered that things such as paraffin oil, nails and string cannot be produced by the animals, that they must go outside the Farm to get them. Napoleon announces that the animals are to begin trading with the humans for these things, especially for the machinery of the windmill. When some of the animals protest that they remember agreeing never to have any dealings with men, Squealer quiets them by pointing out that no such rule has been *written down*, and that the idea of such a ban is simply another of Snowball's lies.

The humans are willing to trade, through an agent, with Animal Farm. They have certain respect for its efficiency, though they still hate it.

At this time, the pigs move into the farmhouse. Squealer explains this move as being necessary to the dignity of Napoleon, as well as to the "brainwork" of the pigs. At the same time, the commandment forbidding animals to sleep in a bed is altered by adding the words "with sheets."

During the autumn (after a rather poor harvest) the animals struggle to complete the windmill. In a violent November storm, however, the half-finished building falls. Napoleon blames Snowball for plotting the destruction and announces that the animals must labor all winter to rebuild the windmill.

Commentary

Orwell's use of point of view enables him here to show very effectively the way in which the rule of Napoleon affects the animals on the farm. Since they no longer participate in or even discuss the decisions made about their lives, their reactions have to do with their personal comfort or discomfort and their measuring of their present lives against what they remember of the past. Few are as willing to accept every edict from Napoleon as enthusiastically as Boxer does. It is mainly a matter of their accepting, more or less, what comes along. Some are puzzled that the past is made to seem different from what they remember, but their memories are hazy and they have to depend on the written commandments and what Squealer tells them. Always they are faced with the choice, usually put by

Squealer, of accepting Napoleon's leadership or allowing Jones to take over again.

They make the only choice that seems possible. None (except, perhaps, the cynical Benjamin) realizes that they have more or less become slaves; they still believe that their victory over men automatically means they are working to build better lives for themselves and their children.

As do all dictators, Napoleon establishes a personal life-style to which everything in the community must contribute. Whim and the need to make the governed constantly respond dictate most of what Napoleon does: moving into the farmhouse, insisting that the windmill be built and rebuilt, encouraging the use of titles when others address him. Every part of life becomes a matter of state, making the dictator's hold over his people more firm and, whenever possible, his personal life more pleasant.

Orwell shows how even the animals' need to end their total isolation from the humans becomes helpful to Napoleon. The Leader "volunteers" to take the "burden" of dealing with human beings on himself. The tone is obviously ironic; Napoleon actually relishes the thought of contact with humans. He resembles a self-seeking opportunist who feels himself superior to his peers and looks to mingle in higher society. All the pigs, for that matter, are widening the line between themselves and the rank-and-file masses. To put it another way, they are becoming just a new order of capitalists "exploiting" the workers as much — or more — than did farmer Jones.

One subject on which Orwell has very strong feelings — the revision of history to make it conform to present needs of political leaders — becomes important in this chapter in the rewritten commandment and the decision to trade with human beings. (Orwell would come back to this theme again, in greater detail, in *1984*.) The past, after all, exists only as it is remembered or recorded. Anyone who is in the position to rewrite history can control both the past and the future. Throughout the story, commandments are revised, one by one, to rationalize what Napoleon decides to do. Having no source for these commandments but the wall of the barn, the animals are forced to accept the changes as they are mysteriously made.

The two-year plan for the building of the windmill and subsequent plans are primarily tools by which Napoleon can maintain his power. If the projects actually work, so much the better, but their real purpose is to keep the masses engaged on such laborious and lengthy projects that they have little time to think. Such projects also give the animals constant occasions (under the pressure of propaganda) to perform heroically and to feel they are contributing to their own good. And the scapegoat — here Snowball — keeps the animals in perpetual fear of an enemy who may undo them at any moment. Only the all-powerful leader can save them from the enemy, the imaginary figure the leader himself has created.

It is all a part of Napoleon's plan to create a reality in Animal Farm that corresponds to his wishes. This special reality is, and must be, an integral part of any totalitarian system. It must not merely be better than any other society; it must also be different so as to increase the isolation in which the society exists. The greater the isolation, the easier it is for the omnipotent leader to maintain his godlike stature. This is part of Orwell's theme in the novel: in a dictatorship, man no longer exists as an individual: only the leader exists as a separate entity, and the masses are but extensions of him.

The farmhouse and the windmill become symbols in the novel, used to support the satire and to underline the theme, as well as advance the plot. The farmhouse is all of the evils and luxuries, unjustly gained, connected with men who hold power. When the pigs decide to live in the farmhouse — which Napoleon does to satisfy his whim of taking over a visible seat of power — their eventual identity with Jones and other human beings is foreshadowed. For Snowball, the windmill was a sign of the enlightened progress for which the community of Animal Farm was founded. For Napoleon, it is a means by which the masses can be kept busy indefinitely. To the other animals it is a barely understood symbol of the better life to which they all aspire. With it as a dream and the idea of a single scapegoat — Snowball — as the only obstacle to achieving it, they become more determined and more loyal to the dictator. Their wills and whatever intelligence they possess have been turned off, and the dictator can use their enthusiasm as one more tool to control them.

Glossary

Arable land—land on which crops are or can be grown.

Broker—a middleman or agent in business.

Governess cart—a light two-wheeled carriage drawn by a horse.

Hedges—a series of thickly-growing bushes or low trees.

Leader—the title assumed by several modern dictators, including Hitler, Mussolini, and Franco (though not Stalin).

Paraffin oil—oil distilled from petroleum, used for lamps and heating, like naphtha.

Solicitor—one kind of lawyer in the two-tiered British system; he advises clients but does not plead in court.

"Two-year plan" for the windmill—a clear reference to Soviet Russia's first Five-Year Plan (originally suggested by Trotsky and put into effect by Stalin in 1928). An attempt to industrialize Russia rapidly, it was a failure and in conjunction with the nationalization of agriculture led to famine and other terrible suffering for the people.

CHAPTER 7
Winter Difficulties and the Trial

Summary

The winter weather is so cold that work on the windmill comes to a temporary halt. In January a shortage of food develops, which the animals conceal from the human beings outside by fooling them into believing that nearly empty bins are full. Soon, though, it becomes necessary to buy grain for food. Squealer announces that to pay for it the hens must supply four hundred eggs a week for sale. When the hens rebel, Napoleon has them starved into submission, but not before nine have died.

For this difficulty, like anything that goes wrong on the farm, Snowball is blamed. In fact, claims Squealer, secret documents have been found proving that Snowball was a traitor and an agent of Jones from the beginning. When Boxer protests that he remembers how bravely Snowball fought in the Battle of the Cowshed, Squealer convinces Boxer that he is mistaken (but the pigs do not forgive Boxer).

A few days later, Napoleon orders all the animals to assemble and announces there are spies and enemy agents in their midst. To everyone's surprise, his dogs seize four of the pigs. They confess to being Jones' agents and in league with Snowball. The dogs tear out their throats. Then the dogs attack Boxer, who easily fends them off. He obeys Napoleon's order to let them go, not realizing that it was Napoleon who had ordered the attack. Many other animals confess and are executed.

After this bloody purge, the working animals move fearfully to the hill overlooking the Farm and look down on it in sorrow. Something has gone wrong with their world, which they have worked so hard to create. Boxer believes that the fault lies in themselves and that they can relieve their sense of guilt only by working harder. But Clover sees that the ideal society they had hoped for, one in which the animals would live in freedom, equality and peace, has been replaced by a world of fear and suspicion.

Unable to put her insight into words, Clover tries to express her feelings by leading the other animals in a mournful rendition of "Beasts of England." But Squealer soon announces that this song is no longer necessary: the new society which it described has arrived. He supplies another song, which praises Animal Farm.

Commentary

Like any dictator, Napoleon must prove his power by making others suffer. Hence, his purge, like those in Stalin's Russia in the mid-1930s. Upon the pretext of a rebellious attitude, four pigs are made to confess and are executed. The call for the truth from Napoleon sets off a wave of hysterical confessions of guilt and immediate executions. It is not that Napoleon really fears the rather feeble shows of discontent that are now cropping up from time to time. Neither do any of the pigs really seem to threaten his leadership. Rather, his dictatorship must be fed by making his power visible and felt and by instilling terror into all subjects, innocent or guilty.

The animals do not understand what is happening. They are shocked by the vicious executions, as well as by the confessions, but Boxer's determination to work harder is typical of their reaction. There is little else they can do.

Napoleon, at this stage, also becomes more and more eccentric personally. He appears only with due ceremony and only surrounded by his bodyguard of vicious dogs. He is making himself inaccessible; the more power is desired and exercised, the more mysterious it needs to become. A god, after all, cannot mingle too often with his people, or the latter may find reason not to believe in his omnipotence.

In the structure of the novel, the animals' gathering on the knoll after the executions is an intended parallel, with the first time the animals gathered there and looked upon their own land, just after the Rebellion. Clover tries to recall the time of the Rebellion when hopes were high, and she is sad that they have not achieved what they set out to do. The purges are wrong, but her conclusion does not mean that she will be disobedient to Napoleon.

The substitution of another song for "Beasts of England" is the replacing of a nostalgic one by one more nationalistic in character. Later, the official poet, Minimus, will produce works extolling the almost sacred qualities of their leader, Napoleon. Like all official songs, the new one is largely ignored by the animals; what moves them is the old one, so closely associated with the Rebellion. It continues to have an underground life in spite of official pronouncements against it by Napoleon.

In both Clover's poignant thoughts and the animals' clinging to "Beasts of England," Orwell seems to be saying that it is far easier to dream of a new order than to achieve it, that such dreams are vain if there is no corresponding change of heart on the part of all concerned. The irony is that what is happening on Animal Farm is the exact opposite to what the Rebellion was all about. The dream was the equality and freedom of a perfect democracy; the reality is the terror and deprivation of to-talitarianism.

Glossary

Black Minorca pullets—young hens of a popular breed for egg-laying.

Clutch—a set of eggs.

Coccidiosis—a contagious disease of poultry.

Mangels—a kind of beetroot used for cattle feed.

Pullet—a young hen.

"Tale of confessions and executions"—a clear reference to Stalin's five great "show trials" of 1936 to 1938, when groups of Party officials were tried for deviationism and plotting with enemy agents. They surprised the world by confessing and were put to death immediately. Some ten years after Orwell wrote *Animal Farm*, it was proved that the "free" confessions were the result of brainwashing and torture.

CHAPTER 8
Napoleon the Leader; the Battle of the Windmill

Summary

The farm animals begin to question the executions as contrary to the commandment which forbids one animal to kill another. But they find that this commandment on the wall now reads ". . . without cause." The work of the animals on the farm and on the windmill now becomes more difficult than ever before. Meanwhile, Napoleon withdraws himself from the other animals and becomes an almost deified leader figure. He is seen only on special occasions, in procession; he takes private apartments in the farmhouse and he is given such titles as "Father of all Animals," and "Terror of Mankind."

Negotiating for the sale of the timber to Pilkington and Frederick, Napoleon announces that he will sell to Pilkington, because of the rumors that Frederick is about to invade Animal Farm and that Frederick treats his own animals cruelly. When the windmill building is finally completed and the machinery for it must be bought, Napoleon reveals that he will sell the timber to Frederick after all. He has pitted the two farmers against one another and forced Frederick to raise his price. He adds that the rumors about Frederick are untrue after all, and that Pilkington, not Frederick, is the animals' enemy. The sale goes through, and the animals discover too late that the banknotes with which Frederick paid are counterfeit. At this moment Frederick does launch an attack on Animal Farm after all.

This attack is the most serious threat of all, because the men use guns and gain control of the whole farmyard. (Pilkington understandably refuses to help the animals.) The men blow up the windmill with dynamite. The sight of the ruin of all their hard labor inspires the animals to drive off the men, though at the cost of many wounded and dead animals. Boxer himself is wounded in this fight, which is named the Battle of the Windmill. The animals then proclaim a celebration, during which the affair of the banknote swindle is conveniently forgotten.

Only a few days later the pigs discover a case of whiskey, and have a further celebration. Their drunken spree has uncomfortable results, after which the commandment forbidding the drinking of alcohol is found to read: ". . . to excess."

Commentary

The Battle of the Windmill is quite another matter from either the Battle of the Cowshed or the Rebellion itself. This latest battle is another sign in the structure of the novel that the story is in the stage of falling. Despair has replaced surprise and hope. It is only the deep affection the animals feel for the Farm, as well as their fury at the cruelty of the attackers, that makes Boxer and the others fight so bravely; Napoleon's frantic screaming is shown to have little real effect.

Following, as it does, so closely on the purges, the Battle, with its destruction of the windmill, is another step in the shattering of the animals' dreams. Yet, although their fight accomplished nothing more than the retaining of their own land while losing the object of two years' backbreaking labor, the Battle is proclaimed by the Leader in celebrations both festive and solemn as a great victory.

Here and throughout the chapter, Orwell's irony is heavy if bitterly humorous. Napoleon's systematic lying is made apparent to the reader but the animals do not catch on. More commandments are rewritten to justify (after the fact) the actions Napoleon takes, and not even finding Squealer in circumstances suggesting (to the reader) that he is the one who changes the commandments on the barn causes the animals to question anything they are told. The discrediting of Snowball continues, as it must in order to enhance Napoleon's "image." The attempt to blacken his character so completely does raise doubts in the minds of some animals but not enough to cause them to question what they are told. The negotiations with the neighboring farms of Foxwood and Pinchfield are transparent attempts by Napoleon to play one farmer against another, but they are only obvious to the reader. Lie succeeds lie, with Squealer sent out to pacify the animals as needed.

Propaganda and its uses are, of course, one of the great targets of criticism in Orwell's satire. Of the most important incidents used in this chapter, Squealer's justifications of Napoleon's actions are most successful. Other instances are less so. For example, the titles Napoleon assumes (for which he is himself obviously the inventor) seem to impress only his fellow pigs. Likewise, the poem dedicated to Napoleon is so clearly a part of a propaganda effort that many animals do not take it very seriously. Its praise of the great leader is too tasteless even for the dullest of the animals on the farm. Still, enough of the propaganda works, and Old Major's vision of the good life so persists that most of the animals are unwilling or unable to see Animal Farm as anything but good, even though they may not even have as much to eat as they did when Jones ran the farm.

In a dictatorship, the manipulation of thought and belief must be constant. Human nature, if left alone, will react to hollow-sounding words in the way Benjamin does. Napoleon must make his power constantly felt by every animal, so he keeps "truth" firmly in his own hands; whether it bears any resemblance to reality, he shapes it to suit his purposes. The result is ultimate absurdity, for without the reality of truth, fixed values disintegrate, everything is arbitrary, and reality itself is made the product of one man's will. Man loses his birthright: the freedom to be.

Glossary
Bottom of the field—the farthest end of the field.

Crown Derby Dinnerware—heirloom porcelain dishes (dating from the eighteenth century) with well-known crown pattern.

Five-pound notes—bills worth about fifteen dollars each (a British pound was worth about three United States dollars when Orwell wrote).

Fortnight—two weeks.

Nightshade berries—belladonna, a highly poisonous perennial herb that grows wild in parts of England.

Title-deeds—documents proving ownership to property.

"Less figures and more food"—a reference to the 1930's fondness of the Soviet government for publishing almost endless statistics designed to impress other countries with Russia's progress. During the period there were actually some years of famine, and most of the published figures were inflated.

CHAPTER 9

Disappearance of Equality and Freedom

Summary

Boxer's wounds heal slowly, and he is growing older. He attempts, nevertheless, to work at the windmill as if he were still young and healthy, concealing his exhaustion and pain so as to get most of the windmill completed before his retirement on pension (as he thinks). The following winter is a hard one, and the animals' rations are reduced several times — except those of the pigs and dogs. Furthermore, thirty-one new pigs are born, and Napoleon insists they must be well fed and educated. A new schoolroom is planned and the materials for its construction must be purchased. The work on the windmill continues, and machinery must be bought.

To help the working animals forget their hard life, the pigs arrange compulsory "spontaneous demonstrations" for them, with flags, speeches and processions. At the same time, the pigs insist on preferential treatment from the other animals. Animal Farm is declared a Republic, and Napoleon is the only candidate in the election for its first President. The distance between the pigs and the other animals continues to grow, while life for the working animals comes to resemble more and more their conditions under Jones. In the summer, Moses the Raven, who has been absent since the Rebellion, returns to preach about Sugarcandy Mountain. Many of the animals believe him, because such a hope for the future makes their lives on the Farm more bearable. The Raven is given a pension by the pigs, although they insist that his stories are lies. Squealer releases written "proof" that Snowball worked with the humans from the beginning of the Revolution; most of the other animals now have only vague memories of him and find it easy to believe what they know they dare not argue against.

Boxer, whose wounds have finally healed, works so hard at the windmill that he overtaxes himself and falls ill. The pigs promise to send him to the veterinarian in town, and Boxer looks forward to recovery and retirement. Instead, he is carted to the slaughter house. The other animals are informed by the pigs that Boxer has died in the hospital despite the best of attention and has been buried with honors, but Benjamin, who was able to read the sign on the cart, knows better and tells the others the truth. The hypocritical pigs hold a memorial banquet for Boxer, at which they drink a case of whiskey, which they have bought with the proceeds from the sale of Boxer.

Commentary

One purpose of this chapter is to show further contemptible measures used by the totalitarian state to tighten the reins on the people. Many of them are psychological manipulations of words and events. Squealer does not report a "reduction" of rations for the animals, only an innocuous "readjustment." According to his "reliable" figures, the food supply now is certainly more ample than in the days of Jones. Even if it weren't, he says, the animals lived in servitude then, but not any more. The *illusion* of freedom is Squealer's unfailing device. The animals must be made to feel that they are enjoying unprecedented well-being, that they are moving closer to the ideals of the Rebellion, and that their leader has the omniscience of a god and even more dedication to the cause than a tireless worker such as Boxer.

The pigs, despite frequent mistakes and apparent reversals, are successful in keeping the illusion going. One reason is the introduction of several distractions from the true state of affairs. The animals cannot understand why Moses is allowed to return and to remain on the farm. The reader can see, of course, exactly why he is tolerated. So long as the animals listen to his tales of Sugarcandy Mountain, where life is better, they will think and complain less often about the hard life they are enduring. Napoleon makes practical use of the argument of Marx, who thought religion is the opiate of the people. Moses is harmless so long as he doesn't interfere with Napoleon's plans for the animals.

Another powerful distraction is the use of more occasions of state to allow the animals to celebrate and, moreover, to make them feel they have reason to celebrate. If their minds are occupied, they will not think of their hunger. One of these events is ironically called Spontaneous Demonstration — ironically because it is preconceived and virtually demanded of the animals. In the last chapter, there was a pronounced reshaping of reality by the pigs. Now history is totally distorted. History has nothing to do with fact but is whatever the leader wants it to be. And the animals, trained to be ignorant, accept what is told to them. Power is complete with this appalling credulity and blind obedience.

The other significant part of this chapter is Orwell's careful treatment of Boxer's sad end. The reader has come to admire Boxer for his strength and self-denying dedication to the farm and also to pity him for his hopeless ignorance and gullibility. He is so good that he is unable to suspect evil in others. That he is to be considered a very remarkable individual is exemplified in the reaction of Benjamin. To the point of Boxer's accident, the wise old donkey displays absolutely no emotion about anything that happens. But when Boxer falls, it is Benjamin who helps him. And when he sees the sign on the truck, he becomes excited, obviously deeply hurt, thus winning the reader's love in addition to respect.

Boxer's plight is not only pathetic, it is also one of the saddest ironies of the novel. He is used by the pigs and then discarded when he is no longer able to work. His loyalty and his devotion to hard work and to whatever Napoleon says are admired by the animals and praised by Napoleon. The reader can see that Orwell intends to show the huge differences among Boxer's idea of himself, the other animals' idea of him, and the role he plays for Napoleon as one more cog in the machine. The animals are shocked when they realize that Boxer has been sold by the pigs to the glue factory; what they don't understand at the time is that he has been used all along.

Boxer's position is important because, in many ways, he represents the masses of Animal Farm. None of the animals other than the pigs really knows until the very end of the novel that Animal Farm is really Manor Farm with a new name. Full of Old Major's vision, they are easy prey for an individual of ambition such as Napoleon.

Many things in this chapter signal the fact that the structure of the novel has reached the stage of rapid fall. Certainly Napoleon's having himself elected president of the Republic of Animal Farm is one. Another is Napoleon's keeping the young pigs apart from the other animals, in both education and normal social contact. He is making Animal Farm into a class society with two groups: the ruling class, with privileges, special education, luxuries and honors; the workers, with the privilege of performing their jobs without complaint and without reward, sometimes even without sufficient food. Napoleon is more and more like Jones all the time.

Glossary

Gill—a liquid measure equal to half a cup.

Knacker—a horse slaughterer and glue maker.

Mash—boiled barley. It is used to feed animals or (as in this case) fermented to make beer.

Piebald—of a mottled color; especially a horse of an irregular black and white coloring.

Poultices—medicinal applications to a wound.

CHAPTER 10

The Final Change

Summary

A number of years have passed, and many of Animal Farm's old inhabitants have died, although Napoleon, Squealer, Clover, Benjamin, and Moses the Raven remain. The farm is more prosperous, but none of the animals has been retired — Clover, for example, is two years beyond retirement age. The windmill has at last been completed, though it is operating a mill for profit and not generating electricity for the animals' comfort. Napoleon has substituted for that dream the ideal of frugality. The life of the working animal is now exactly as it had been before the Rebellion, yet the new generation does not know the past at all, and the remaining old-timers can barely remember it; neither has anything with which to compare the present. Their one consolation is that they, and not humans, own the farm, and they hope for the freedom of the whole country from man.

On the other hand, the increasing numbers of pigs and dogs are enjoying the farm's prosperity. And at this point the final transformation of the pigs begins. First, the pigs begin to walk on their hind legs, carrying whips. To get around the old summary of the Commandments, "Four legs good, two legs bad," the sheep are trained to bleat over and over "Four legs good, two legs better," drowning out all protests. The commandment reading "All animals are equal" is changed as well; the pigs have added: ". . . but some animals are more equal than others." All the pigs adopt human clothes, buy a radio, install a telephone, and so on.

The final scene in the book describes a party to which the pigs have invited the neighboring humans. In a brief speech, Napoleon announces that the pigs, as the owners of the farm, wish only to live in economic and social peace with their human neighbors and that many of the animals' "foolish customs" are due for a change, including renaming the place back to "Manor Farm." The other animals, looking on from outside, see the pigs' faces beginning to change. When the pigs and humans begin to quarrel, the other animals finally realize that the pigs and humans look exactly alike, that it is impossible to say which is which.

The shocking but inevitable transformation of the pigs into humans is complete. There is, symbolically, no difference between the former masters and the new dictators of the Farm.

Commentary

It is especially clear at the end of the novel why Orwell chose the point of view he did. Throughout the story the reader understands what the animals do not because he has the advantage of a greater range of vision. The animals understand only so much as they are able to see. This in itself is a demonstration of why they allow Napoleon to work against their welfare. Their discovery of the truth about the society of Animal Farm, in the scene in which they watch the pigs and the human beings together in the farmhouse, is made to seem very real and is affecting to the reader in spite of his superior knowledge. Orwell is convincing: the animals really are full of good will but are deceived, sold out.

The logic of the plot requires that human beings appear at the end of the novel. They provide the circumstances in which it is shown that Napoleon has become indistinguishable from Jones. The kind of prosperity which Animal Farm achieves is accomplished in the same way as Jones, had he been more diligent and disciplined, might have used: at the expense of the animals.

The fall of the structure is now complete. The pigs look like human beings. Animal Farm is once again Manor Farm, and the animals are looking in from outside. Everything is as it was, except for one thing: the animals have experienced freedom but it has been taken away.

The change in the pigs is symbolized in several ways: their walking erect on two feet and wearing human clothes, Napoleon's carrying a whip — that dreaded symbol of human oppression — the pigs and human beings mingling socially in the farmhouse, their drinking toasts and playing cards, indeed, their distrusting each other over the game of cards. In short, the pigs have put on almost all the physical and social characteristics of man.

All the Commandments have now been modified to the point of being meaningless. Their summary is a summary of Orwell's satirical point, as well as being his most famous line: "All animals are equal, but some animals are more equal than others."

What began as utopia, as heaven on earth, has ended as the opposite. As Orwell seems to say, good will, good intentions, ideals, common decency are not enough, although they should be. Something in human nature or the human condition prevents man from ever regaining paradise, as it were. Orwell himself would probably not put it this way. He would perhaps echo the famous statement of Lord Acton: "Power corrupts, and absolute power corrupts absolutely."

Glossary

Daily Mirror—a very popular London daily morning newspaper.

Dog-cart—a two-wheeled horse-drawn cart.

John Bull—a British weekly magazine aimed at a family readership.

Ratcatcher breeches—unconventional, full-cut pants worn by professional ratcatchers.

Tit-bits—a London weekly newspaper, geared for instruction and amusement of a mass audience.

Watered silk—silk material with a wavy finish.

Wardrobes—cupboards, bureaus.

Wireless set—a radio.

Animal Farm as Satire

When *Animal Farm* first appeared, it was taken entirely as a satire on the history of the Soviet Union: the Marxist Revolution, Stalin's rise to power, and the attitudes and actions of various Western nations. Orwell was convinced that the Marxist Revolution of 1917 had been betrayed by Stalin. This conviction was soon shown to be perfectly justified for Stalin's lack of respect and regard for truth, consistency, moral principles and human life was made abundantly clear in all of his actions. However, no one had the courage to condemn Russia in 1943 because she was fighting bravely against Germany and delaying the feared attack on England. Orwell's greatest fear was that people would now forget what had happened in the immediate past, and he wrote *Animal Farm* to make sure that his fear would not be realized.

Perhaps the easiest way to explain the satire is to retell the story, showing the most important parallels. Manor Farm (Russia) is run by Mr. Jones (the Tsar), a man more absorbed in whiskey and his own creature comforts than in caring for his livestock (the Russian people). The farm animals, knowing no other life, are aroused only after a stirring deathbed speech from Old Major (Marx, Lenin), the patriarch boar. His thesis is that Man (capitalists) exploits the animals, taking for himself the product of their work and giving them in return a bare subsistence level of food and care. Get rid of man, he says, and all animals will lead a new full life. He bids them to prepare for rebellion and then teaches them the song, "Beasts of England" (the "Internationale"), depicting the glorious days of freedom and riches when "tyrant man" is overthrown.

Revolutionary activities begin in secret (the two decades or so preceding the Revolution), led by the pigs, who gave the name Animalism (Communism) to the philosophical system they elaborate from Major's thesis. Their chance to act comes unexpectedly. On a day of worse-than-usual neglect (World War I), they break into the food bins; and when Jones and his men (the White army) show up with ships, the animals turn on them spontaneously and drive them off the farm (the Revolution of 1917). Mrs. Jones (the Russian nobility and court hangers-on) takes flight as well, followed by Moses the Raven (organized religion).

The animals, in an ecstasy of joy at their independence, set about running the farm themselves. The leaders are the pigs, who have taught themselves to read and write, and manage to teach some of the others (the educational efforts of the early Bolsheviks, especially Trotsky). The name Manor Farm (Russia) is changed to Animal Farm (Soviet Union), and the Seven Commandments of Animalism are painted on the wall of the barn. The first summer is one of success; the animals work hard, live well, and take tremendous pride in overcoming their difficulties. The animals (proletariat) do not realize for some time that the pigs (Party members) are gradually eating more and working less than the others.

At the regular Sunday meetings (a composite of the many collective efforts of the early days after the Revolution) the whole group gathers to plan the week's work and make all decisions, but the pigs generally seem to hold the floor — especially two young boars: Snowball (Trotsky) and Napoleon (Stalin). Their enmity soon becomes clear. The third most important pig is Squealer (*Pravda* and all propaganda efforts) who can always convince the other animals that the privileges usurped by the pigs are solely for the good of the farm.

Meanwhile, on the neighboring farms, all sorts of rumors circulate about Animal Farm. Because Pilkington of Foxwood (the Western Allies, especially England) and Frederick of Pinchfield (Germany) do not get along with each other, no concerted offensive is staged against Animal Farm. Jones, aided by Frederick and a band of other men, attack in the fall, but Snowball's leadership and careful strategy enable the animals to push them back. After this Battle of the Cowshed (the half-hearted anti-revolutionary efforts of the West to reinstate the Tsar), medals are conferred on Snowball and Boxer (the peasantry), whose strength and loyalty are the backbone of the new order.

With winter comes hunger (the bitter winters of 1917-18 and 1918-19 with the country in chaos) and there are now defections. Mollie, the vain and pretty carriage horse (the comfort-loving bourgeoisie) vanishes from the farm to pull an attractive cart in town (the numerous middle class who fled the Revolution for the West). The cat (an industrialist) disappears at work time and reappears at feeding time. The others work hard and follow the rules, although Benjamin (the cynic) maintains his quiet philosophy that nothing will change.

The power struggle reaches a climax over the question of the windmill (industrialization), for which Snowball makes detailed plans. Napoleon sneers at the idea and when the question comes to a vote at the Sunday meeting, he suddenly summons nine huge, fierce dogs (secret police). Snowball flees and Napoleon assumes complete control (as did Stalin after Lenin's death).

Surrounded by his dogs, he at once announces that a committee of pigs (commissars) will make all decisions henceforth. All protests are effectively silenced by the snarling dogs, the sheep (the masses) bleating propaganda slogans, and by Squealer's explanation of Napoleon's self-sacrifice in assuming leadership and relieving the less gifted animals of the danger of making wrong decisions (the beginnings of Stalin's "cult of personality").

When Napoleon subsequently announces plans (the first five-year plan) to build the windmill after all, Squealer explains: "tactics, comrades, tactics!" The plan had been Napoleon's all along; he merely appeared to oppose it in order to get rid of Snowball, a dangerous traitor — or so says Squealer (the denouncing of Trotskyites).

As time goes on, work somehow takes longer and becomes harder, and rations are shorter (the famines of the first five-year plan), in spite of

Squealer's impressive statistics on production (Soviet propoganda throughout the 1920s and 1930s). The Commandments also seem to have become less decisive; qualifying words are there which the animals cannot remember having seen before, but Squealer can always convince them of their faulty memories (the corruption of Marxism).

The windmill is started with tremendous effort, but it collapses in a windstorm (the failure of the first five-year plan). While the animals double their efforts to rebuild it, Napoleon announces that Animal Farm will engage in trade with neighboring farms in order to get necessities the Farm cannot produce (Soviet Russia's resumption of trade with the West in the 1930s).

And so it goes. The animals work even harder while the pigs move into the farmhouse using beds, dishes and all the rest of the supposedly outlawed human contrivances (Party officials' assumption of privileges). Snowball is declared to have plotted with Jones from the first; the history of the Rebellion and the Battle of the Cowshed is reworded to confirm this (the revision of history under Stalin).

Soon after, the hens are ordered to give up all their eggs for sale to humans. They smash their eggs rather than obey (the Kulaks' [middle-class farmers] reaction to the first five-year plan). They are starved into submission (Stalin's suppression of the Kulaks).

Napoleon holds court, and four pigs confess to being in league with Snowball or otherwise sabotaging the farm — for which they have their throats torn out by the dogs (the blood purges of the 1930s).

As for trade with humans, Napoleon vacillates between Frederick and Pilkington (as Stalin did with Germany and other countries of Europe before World War II). At last, Napoleon announces that he is selling some timber to Frederick (The Nazi-Soviet nonagression pact) in order to pay for having machinery installed in the newly completed windmill. But Frederick pays in counterfeit banknotes, and soon afterward attacks Animal Farm (Hitler's sudden invasion of Russia), blowing up the precious windmill. In a rage, the animals drive off the men, but several are killed and many wounded. Nevertheless, Squealer declares the Battle of the Windmill a glorious victory (World War II, which was still being fought on Russian soil when the book was written).

The pigs continue to fatten while the rations of the others decrease. New decrees issue from the farmhouse. The hungry animals are held in control by "Spontaneous Demonstrations" (a typical Communist propaganda device) celebrating the success and prosperity of the farm, and Moses, the raven, suddenly reappears (the return of the church following its earlier suppression in Russia).

Then Boxer falls ill, and is carted away in a vehicle marked "Horse Slaughterer and Glue Boiler." His death in a hospital is announced three days later. This is another example of the authorities withholding information and then revealing it as it suits their purposes.

The windmill is rebuilt (rapid, enforced industrial build-up in Russia), and the Farm prospers, but somehow only the pigs and dogs seem to benefit. Even the plan to spread the Rebellion throughout England (the Comintern) has been outlawed by Napoleon. Few of the original revolutionaries are left to remember the old days.

At last, the day comes when the pigs appear walking on two legs, and the sheep have mysteriously changed their chant to "Four legs good, two legs better." The pigs wear clothes now, and carry whips as they supervise the farm work. The Seven Commandments on the barn wall have been reduced to just one: "All animals are equal, but some animals are more equal than others."

A group of farmers, led by Pilkington, come to the farm for a party (the Teheran Conference, when Stalin met with the leaders of the Western Allies). But a violent quarrel (the Cold War, though it had not yet happened when Orwell wrote the book) breaks out over a game of cards. When the other animals peer in, to see what is happening, they find that they cannot distinguish between the men and the pigs (the growing resemblance of Russian Communism to Western capitalism).

Characterization

Limitations

Orwell's choice of the fable form places great limitations on his characters. In most fictional works, a character is not meant to represent anything or anybody in the real world; he or she is simply an individual and can show the kind of quirks and surprising responses that make each person unique. In fable, however, the personality of each character must conform to his or her role in the allegory, and nothing can intrude to distract the reader from the lesson. The form almost demands flat, one-dimensional characters, each of whom represents a particular human quality. In *Animal Farm*, one character sometimes represents several qualities, but the combination is never surprising. Boxer is loyal *and* patient, Mollie is vain *and* comfort-seeking. Once the main quality for each character is chosen, he or she must be drawn very simply and in such a way as to emphasize that trait, like a cartoon. The characters' motivations for their actions must be implicit in what they are, and no character change is possible.

Orwell's task of allegorical characterization was made more difficult by his use of animals. First, the designation of a particular animal for each character had to have some logic yet serve the satirical purpose. The choice of the pigs, for example, is brilliant; they are general symbols of greed and self-indulgence, yet they are intelligent animals, and it is even possible — by a long stretch of the imagination — for the reader to pretend that they are capable of the actions they take. Chickens or cows, say, would not serve nearly so well. In addition, to maintain any believability, the author must combine in each character convincing details of animal behavior with a recognizable, if simplified human personality.

Another problem in *Animal Farm* was the necessity of the characters' illustrating the history of Soviet Russia. The personality and actions of each character had to contribute to this throughout. In the case of those characters meant to be identified as specific, well-known persons, some attention also had to be paid to historical accuracy. The author could, of course, use what is called "historical licence" — the omission, simplification, and rearranging of details to further the story — but too many changes would have destroyed the allegory.

Effects

Despite these limitations, Orwell's characterization is remarkable. Although he could not *develop* characters as the author of a traditional novel does, he achieved an interesting effect by slowly *revealing* the personalities of such characters as Napoleon, Squealer, and Boxer. Even minor characters, such as Benjamin, show more of themselves as the plot unfolds, though there are never any surprises. Small, quick details (often understated) are used to create convincing portraits. They are familiar cartoons but they have far more specificity and personality than the characters in many allegories, more, perhaps, than those in much second-rate "realistic" fiction. Moreover, Orwell was able to evoke emotional reactions to his characters. Squealer is detestable, Boxer is admirable and lovable. The reader cares about what happens to them, and reacts to the characters themselves, not only to the incidents involving them. This is a considerable achievement for a fable.

Character Sketches

Old Major

Old Major is Orwell's satiric portrait of Marx. Major preaches the ideals of revolutionary socialism in their pure form. He introduces and details the principles of the Rebellion which will be elaborated into the Seven Commandments and the philosophy of Animalism by the other pigs. Orwell portrays him sympathetically from the very start: "Old Major was so highly regarded on the farm that everyone was quite ready to lose an hour's sleep in order to hear what he had to say." Major's speech confirms the animals' good opinion of him. He is a revolutionary, but a humane and sympathetic one. In this, Orwell has deliberately contrasted him with the post-revolutionary leaders, Napoleon and Snowball. Whereas Snowball (like Major) wants to solve the animals' problems by revolution, he can suggest plans of action, and put these into practice, while Old Major is a theorist and visionary: Major has a dream of the perfect society, and has developed ideas over the years concerning the organization and the laws of this society; but he gives no practical plan for *bringing about* the change. Napoleon is also contrasted with Major. Napoleon does not have the idealistic and public-spirited motives of the other two — he is merely self-centered and selfish, eager and willing to satisfy his private desires.

Major, then, plays a more important role than he seems to. With his sympathy and idealism he provides a contrast to Snowball and Napoleon, showing the possibility of a revolutionary without the failings of these two — to prove that not all rebels are selfish. Of course, at the same time his failure to put his theories into practice contrasts with the other two pigs' ability to plan and act successfully. Orwell here underlines an important fact about revolution: words and theories alone cannot accomplish the desired transformation of society. The great problem is that practical action, which is also necessary, sometimes has unfortunate results; physical action means physical power, and power can be abused as well as used (as Napoleon's actions prove). This is a paradoxical problem which Orwell thinks is very important to state; but he makes no attempt in *Animal Farm* to solve it.

Major's main appearance comes in the first chapter. After his death his memory is revered. His skull is dug up, and the animals pay it a weekly visit of homage. But his ideas are treated increasingly ironically. The last mention of Major comes in Napoleon's speech at the end of the book. Major's idealistic dream of freedom and equality is by now only an embarrassment to Napoleon, who proceeds to rid himself of it. As Napoleon says, "There had been a strange custom, whose origin was unknown, of marching every Sunday morning past a boar's skull which was nailed to a post in the garden. This . . . would be suppressed, and the skull had already been buried."

Major certainly stands for Karl Marx (1818-83), the German

economist whose works with Friedrich Engels are the foundation of modern socialism and of communism. (It is important to remember here that Orwell was an avowed socialist.) His *Communist Manifesto* and *Das Kapital* are based on the idea that economic structure is the basis of all history and determines all aspects of life, social, political, and intellectual. He sees employers and employees (the proletariat) as opposed to each other in every war. Since the evils of capitalism cannot be reformed, the whole of capitalist society, along with its evil economy, must be destroyed by revolution and a new, classless society created. One of Marx's most famous quotations can be heard echoing throughout Major's great speech in Chapter 1: "Workers have nothing to lose in this [revolution] but their chains. They have a world to gain. Workers of the world, unite!"

In some ways Major also represents Nikolai Lenin (born Vladimir Ilyich Ulyanov: 1870-1924), who "translated" the thought of Marx and Engels into reality in Russia by leading the Bolsheviks in the Revolution and serving as head of the new Soviet state until his death. Although he played a considerably more active role in history than Major does in *Animal Farm*, there are many parallels in the way the memory of both was used and misused after their deaths.

In a more general way, Major stands for any great and revolutionary thinker whose ideas can change the world but are liable to change (not necessarily for the better) as they are put into action by those who come after.

Snowball

Orwell says of Snowball that he has "less depth of character" than Napoleon but is more imaginative and inventive. He co-operates with Napoleon and Squealer to organize Major's ideas into the principles of Animalism, and to reduce these to the Seven Commandments. It is Snowball who organizes the various Animal Committees and the classes in reading and writing, thus showing his interest in the other animals (while Napoleon looks on). It is Snowball who compresses the Commandments into the summary, "Four legs good, two legs bad," for the benefit of the less intelligent animals. Snowball also anticipates the first attack on Animal Farm and, having studied up on strategy (at which he seems to excel), he plans the successful defence of the Battle of the Cowshed. At the same time, as a pig of action as well as thought, Snowball is in the middle of the Battle, leading the dangerous first skirmish, fooling the men into an ambush, and turning and leading the last victorious charge, in which he is wounded. He is decorated for his actions.

Snowball wants to preserve the differences between the pigs and the other animals — that is, he does not believe in Major's principle of equality — but he does have a vision, like Major, of a better society for the animals. On the other hand, whereas Major's dream is a simple one of comfort and sufficient food in a country setting, Snowball's dream is of a world of machines; the windmill is the symbol of this world. When Snowball designs and advocates it, Napoleon disagrees, and the debate which follows gives Napoleon the chance to get rid of Snowball. Here, Orwell is repeating the lesson that physical power is more potent than mere intelligence and ingenuity: Snowball pays for his devotion to imaginative schemes by being banished; the opposite qualities, those of single-minded selfishness and cruelty, help Napoleon to power.

Snowball's memory, like Major's, lingers on in Animal Farm, but in a different way: a scapegoat is necessary, someone on whom to blame all the troubles of the Farm, so as to prove that Leader Napoleon can make no mistakes. Like Major's memory, however, Snowball's memory helps to remind the reader of the reality and the ideals of the Revolution, and helps to illustrate the pigs' hypocrisy.

In *Animal Farm*'s symbolism of communist history, Snowball represents Leon Trotsky (Lev Davidovich Bronstein 1879-1940), who worked brilliantly with Lenin in preparing the way for the Russian Revolution and establishing a new society afterward. He was an outstanding organizer and an early advocate of industrialization and of spreading the revolution beyond the borders of Russia. After Lenin's death, Trotsky and Stalin, who already hated each other, opposed each other more vigorously. Eventually Stalin, who was in control of the country, exiled his rival. From France and later Mexico, Trotsky kept up a steady, bitter criticism of Stalin's policies until his assassination (on orders from Stalin) in 1940. Meanwhile, Stalin and his followers blackened Trotsky's name and thought within the country (while adopting several of his ideas); for some time, "Trotskyite" was equivalent to "traitor" in Russia.

In the more general fable, Snowball represents what a revolutionary can be. Orwell admired Trotsky, although he did not agree with him in every way. Some critics believe Snowball is intended as Orwell's only note of hope in the book, that he implies "what might have happened if Snowball had triumphed over Napoleon." Others think that his defeat is pictured as inevitable.

Napoleon

Through the portrait of Napoleon, Orwell makes an important contribution to the understanding of the modern political dictator. The model is especially Stalin. Willing, while it suits him, to support and help lead the revolution, Napoleon only gradually shows his real character as the plot unfolds. In fact, the plot of *Animal Farm* is in one sense the story of Napoleon's rise to power. Orwell describes him at first as "not much of a talker, but with reputation for getting his own way." Orwell adds that Napoleon has more "depth of character" than Snowball, and Orwell is surely using the word "depth" ironically.

In Chapter 2, immediately after the Rebellion, the differences in character between Snowball and Napoleon are already clearly illustrated.

Snowball occupies himself with tasks of social benefit: writing out the Seven Commandments, and organizing the harvest, while Napoleon looks on sourly, and acts only in the last scene of that chapter, to take charge of the milk. Napoleon's greed and self-interest are already apparent.

The differences between Napoleon and Snowball are illustrated again in the third chapter, when Snowball gives a long explanation to satisfy the birds that they also fit into the category of "four legs good" even with their wings. Snowball uses intelligence and logic; Napoleon uses other methods. It is at this time that he takes over the care of the puppies who are to grow into the bodyguard of huge dogs who chase Napoleon's rival, Snowball, off the Farm. Napoleon uses cunning and brute force. He is also cunning enough to understand the value of Squealer's propaganda, and he has no moral scruples against the distortions and plain lies which Squealer uses.

After Snowball is banished, Napoleon takes over control of Animal Farm, abolishing the democratic rights of the animals. At the same time, he withdraws himself from the society of the others, and begins to create an unrealistic image of himself in the animals' minds. On the one hand, he becomes inflated into the image of the traditional "Napoleon" figure — the great Leader: Boxer's repeated lesson is that "Napoleon can do no wrong;" Napoleon is called the "Fountain of Happiness;" and even the hens and cows give him credit for increasing the egg-production and purifying the water. On the other hand, it is Napoleon who originates all the new regulations on the farm, which have the effect of increasing the animals' hardships: for example, the sixty-hour week, and the Sunday work. And it is Napoleon who plans and leads the bloody trials of the animals who question his authority.

As a result of the trials and the new regulations, another image of Napoleon grows — that of a mysterious, powerful, terrifying being. He is feared, but not hated, and the animals obey him without question. For example, even after the first bloody trial, Clover has "no thought of rebellion or disobedience," although she is disappointed and miserable. To summarize, Napoleon projects an image that arouses a mixture of love, awe and fear in the animals, and that he helps to foster by withdrawing himself from them. He becomes the mysterious source of everything that happens to them, both good and evil, a father figure, typical of the modern dictator.

Although Napoleon keeps away from the other animals in the latter part of the book, the reader gradually gathers clues to his character and motives, from the glimpses that Orwell gives of his machinations. He reveals his vain desire for exclusiveness when he takes private apartments in the farmhouse and when he makes a rule that the other animals must step aside when he passes. He demonstrates his murderous cruelty when he leads the executions, when he starves the chickens into submission and when he sends Boxer to the slaughterhouse. He illustrates his hypocrisy by the lie he tells the animals about Boxer's careful treatment and by the changes that are made in the Commandments. His dishonesty and hypocrisy are completely revealed, in the last scene, in his bragging about the animals' miserable conditions (the opposite of Squealer's propaganda to the animals themselves). There are, of course, many other examples.

The last detail to complete the reader's knowledge of Napoleon also comes in the last scene: Napoleon changes from animal to human. The human image here is, of course, the symbol of capitalist oppression; but it is ironic that this image should point an uncomfortable finger at the human reader himself.

Boxer

Orwell describes Boxer as ''an enormous beast . . . as strong as any two ordinary horses . . .; not of first-rate intelligence, but universally respected for his steadiness of character. . . .'' He and his mare, Clover, are ''the most faithful disciples'' of Animalism. Once the involved philosophy is explained to them, the two horses accept it unquestioningly and teach it to the other animals.

As Orwell shows, the physical success of Animal Farm really rests in Boxer's strength and persistence: ''Nothing could have been achieved without Boxer, whose strength seemed equal to that of all the other animals put together.'' He has only two rules: ''Napoleon is always right'' and ''I will work harder.'' He believes most faithfully that all problems can be solved by applying these maxims.

Boxer's compassion is in strong contrast to Napoleon's cruelty. Boxer believes Major's commandment that no animal should kill any other animal — and Boxer extends this to all life. When he has knocked down the stableboy and is afraid he has killed him, Boxer says sorrowfully, ''I have no wish to take life, even human life.''

Boxer is brave enough (or unintelligent enough) to challenge the pigs when he can remember a fact or a rule that they attempt to alter or deny, but Squealer is always a bit too clever for him, and explains away the changes, leaving Boxer's faith in Napoleon undisturbed. Boxer's challenges are not forgotten by the pigs, however. During the first trial, the dogs attack him. But Boxer is too faithful and unintelligent to realize that Napoleon himself has sent the dogs, and he shows his lack of cruelty by letting the dogs free — on order from Napoleon.

Boxer lives out his life in patient and unquestioning service. Finally his illness, caused by overwork, gives the pigs their chance for revenge. Promising him care in the hospital, they have him carted away to the slaughterhouse, exactly the same fate that Major warned him he would suffer under Jones if he did *not* revolt. Only in the last minute does Boxer realize what the pigs have done to him, and his only protest is to kick against the walls of the cart — too weakly and too late.

In considering Boxer, it makes little difference whether one reads *Animal Farm* as a general fable or the history of the Russian Revolution. He represents the ardent, selfless party workers, the idealized masses, and his fate is that of the ordinary, decent-minded worker under any dictatorship.

Clover

Clover is described as a "stout motherly mare approaching middle life. . . ." She is a mother figure and provides a contrast to the inhuman selfishness of the pigs. After Napoleon's first trial and executions, the animals gather instinctively around her, as if to associate with sympathetic feelings at this time of cruel murder.

Clover, like Boxer, is a faithful and trusting believer in Napoleon and Animalism, and an uncomplaining worker. She is intelligent enough to find out that Mollie has been fraternizing with the humans, yet not cruel enough to tell the other animals Mollie's secret. She has sufficient memory and understanding to be able to compare the old life and the hopes of the animals for a better life, with the bitter failure of these hopes after the first trial.

After the death of Boxer, Clover takes over his plot function as the eyes of the ordinary masses through which the failure of the Rebellion is seen. She is the one who questions the pigs' walking on their hind legs, and she makes Benjamin read out the transformed commandment, "Some animals are more equal than others." It is also Clover who, in the last scene, leads the frightened animals into the garden of the farmhouse, where they stare in at the partying pigs and humans. There, it is she who sees the final transformation of the pigs: "Clover's old dim eyes flitted from one face to another . . . it was impossible to say which was which." Sympathy and hope are at this point on the outside looking in on cruelty, vanity and selfishness.

In addition to symbolizing, with Boxer, the common people who are betrayed by the Revolution, Clover represents the sympathetic feelings between individuals that Orwell believes must underlie the creation of the ideal society.

Benjamin

Orwell describes Benjamin the donkey as bad-tempered, untalkative, unlaughing, and, above all, cynical. Some critics of the book have suggested he is difficult to understand; they are obviously not fans of Western movies, in which often appear a minor character who is basically sympathetic but comments cynically on the situation. The difference is, of course, that in *Animal Farm*, it is the cynic who is right.

Benjamin does have sympathetic aspects (besides being the only animal who comes close to achieving the reader's understanding of the situation). He is "devoted" to Boxer, and anyone who is Boxer's friend must have the reader's sympathy. In fact, the only time he ever moves quickly or reveals his feelings is when Boxer is taken away. The shock of his friend's death does not change him, however, it only makes him "more morose and taciturn than ever."

Benjamin is not really so much a cynic as a skeptic and a realist. He is skeptical about the possibility of achieving the paradise of which Major and Snowball dream. In fact, one of Benjamin's functions is to provide a contrast to Major. Where Major is optimistic and theoretical, Benjamin is practical and pessimistic; he believes from the first that the animals' condition will not change despite the Rebellion. For this reason he is not surprised at anything the pigs do, nor is he surprised at the gradual failure of the new society of Animal Farm or the gradual rise of the pigs to power. And while he doesn't shirk, he never does more than his share. Benjamin is, as Orwell says, the oldest animal on the farm; he is older even than Major — and wiser, as it turns out. It is Benjamin's pessimistic attitude towards the possibilities of revolution which is proven correct, and not Major's optimistic one. It is suitable, therefore, that it is Benjamin who reads out the commandment that has been altered to ''Some animals are more equal than others.'' He has never believed that the principle of equality, upon which the rebellion and the new society are based, can be defended against selfish desires.

Generally, Benjamin represents the pessimist, the one who has no faith in social revolution, though he does have deep personal sympathies and friendships. Orwell does not mean to give Benjamin the last word, however; for as he shows, pessimism and skepticism lead to inaction in the face of injustice, and lack of ability even to oppose evil.

Moses the Raven

In the incidents dealing with Moses the Raven, Orwell parallels the history of the Soviet attitude to religion quite closely. Moses follows Jones off the Farm after the Rebellion, just as the Communists persecuted religious institutions after the Revolution (Marx had declared that religious hope for life after death prevented the masses from striving for a better life on earth). Moses returns after Napoleon comes to power and is tolerated by the pigs, just as the Soviet Union began eventually to tolerate the practice of religion, while giving it no special rights. There is more, however, than just this parallel to the depiction of Moses. Orwell describes Moses as a definitely unsympathetic character, thus showing some agreement with Marx's views on organized religion.

Moses is ''a spy and a tale-bearer'' and does no work. Before the Rebellion he lives on the bread and beer that Jones provides; he is really a hireling and agent of Jones. He is clever and, when opposing the pigs' teachings about a paradise on earth, he tries to make the animals believe in the unreal Sugarcandy Mountain. He disappears from the story when the Rebellion occurs and does not reappear until several years later, when he simply takes up where he left off, doing no work and preaching once more about Sugarcandy Mountain. The attitude of the pigs to him is curious: they insist that he preaches lies, but they tolerate him and even give him an allowance of beer to live on. In fact, Moses the Raven's position on Animal

Farm becomes exactly what it has been on Manor Farm under Jones.

Orwell's lesson in the depiction of Moses the Raven is more complex than it seems at first. Orwell makes it clear that Moses has a despicable character; he is a spy and parasite. But Orwell also indicates that he does some good; after the Rebellion is undermined, many of the animals need the hope of Sugarcandy Mountain to make their present lives more bearable. Marx warned against just this function of religion, but Orwell believes that in the absence of hope for heaven-on-earth there is a place for religious hope.

Mollie

Orwell describes Mollie as "the foolish, pretty white mare who drew Mr. Jones' trap." She may be foolish, but she is clever enough to make friends with the human enemy, conceal her actions, and desert Animal Farm without being caught. Mollie is not sympathetic to the other animals because she has never suffered as they have. She has been pampered by Jones and made vain of her good looks. She shows that she doesn't understand Animalism, by asking about her ribbons — she has to be told that ribbons are like clothes, and forbidden to animals. During the Battle of the Cowshed she shows cowardice, hiding during the fight. She is also lazy, doing as little work as possible, and inventing imaginary ailments to avoid it. In the end, she is tempted by ribbons and lump-sugar to desert her comrades on Animal Farm; and when Clover asks her outright if she is friendly with humans, she denies it, proving herself a liar as well. It is no surprise, therefore, when Mollie disappears one day, and goes to work for an innkeeper.

Orwell, in depicting Mollie, wants to illustrate that the cruelty and power-hunger of Napoleon are not the only individual characteristics that help destroy the revolution: Mollie's foolishness, vanity and servile nature are more innocent and more common traits than Napoleon's, but almost as dangerous. Orwell is underlining yet again that an abstract and theoretical ideal cannot take into account individual differences in practice; and that a better society can only be realized if human nature is taken into account.

Squealer

Squealer is the perfect propaganda officer, the ultimate in henchmen. Orwell makes him believable but gives him a sketchier portrait than most of the characters — we are told only that he is a small pig with "twinkling eyes, nimble movements, and a shrill voice . . . when he was arguing . . . he had a way of skipping from side to side and whisking his tail which was somehow very persuasive." This very lack of detailed characterization is telling. He simply does not have much visible personality of his own. His actions are all elaborations of what his master wants.

Squealer accomplishes his ends by talking, and he is brilliant at it. He can prove anything about anything, explain black into white, justify any shift of attitude or rules, and is eventually discovered to be the means by which the written Commandments are changed. Of the founders of Animalism, he is the one who is the talker from the beginning. He helps Snowball write out the Commandments and as early as Chapter 3 is busy explaining, on a scientific basis, that the pigs should receive all the milk and apples to help them in their brain work (lest Jones comes back — his constant threat). His great skill in propaganda is shown, after Snowball's defeat, when he manages to justify Napoleon's reversal on the question of building the windmill. Yet, here, he is ready with a more powerful threat if his words should fail: ''. . . the three dogs who happened to be with him growled so threateningly, that they accepted his explanation without further question.''

After this, as Squealer goes about his duties with relish, explaining away one change after another, he is always accompanied by two or three dogs. This is not the only example of his cowardice; he is in the rear of the Battle of the Cowshed and is ''unaccountably'' missing during the Battle of the Windmill. Had the latter been a defeat, the reader suspects he might have been able to change sides successfully.

An excellent judge of character and the tide of opinion, Squealer misses no opportunity to build up Napoleon's image or incriminate Snowball. He also falls into most of Napoleon's vices: greed, drunkenness, and cruelty (he eventually chooses the victims for ''liquidation'').

In Russian history, Squealer represents the large and active propaganda machine of the Soviet Union. As an individual, however, his career and tactics are closer to those of Joseph Goebbels, Hitler's minister for propaganda. And on the general level, his type is all too well known in many modern countries.

The Humans: Jones, Frederick, Pilkington, Whymper

The human characters, Jones, Frederick, Pilkington and Whymper, play minor roles in the story. There is a good reason for this: in the form which Orwell chose, the animal satire, the story must be told from the point of view of the animals and revolve around then. If the humans intrude too much, then the whole fantasy or illusion of the animal world breaks down, so that animals acting like humans become ridiculous. This is something which Orwell successfully guards against, by keeping the human characters well in the background and giving little or no detail as to their characters, except those necessary to the plot, and the traits typical of the image which they represent.

When human characters do appear, none is pleasant or admirable. This is important, whether men are taken to symbolize capitalists specifically, or oppressors and the status quo in general. Orwell's personal belief was in complete agreement with the requirement of the satire: the revolution is completely justified. Its theory, means and outcome may be questioned, but the need for radical change is there.

Farmer Jones is drawn with the most detail. It is necessary for the plot that he show the traits of cruelty, laziness, drunkenness, moodiness, and bad management of the farm. Having demonstrated these in the first two chapters, he rarely appears again, except as a threat to the animals, kept current by Squealer: "Surely you don't want Jones to return?"

Jones' unpleasant characteristics are needed to provide motivation for the animals' revolt. They are also required by the satire. In one reading, Jones represents the tsars of Russia, specifically the last, Nicholas II (1868-1918). Although convinced of the divine right of kings, he was so weak that he abdicated quite easily when faced with revolt in 1917. He was assassinated in 1918. More important, Jones represents the evil state of the world in general, the *need* for revolution.

Frederick of Pinchfield Farm and Pilkington of Foxwood Farm are even more shadowy figures. They represent both more justification for revolution and the failure of the enemies of the revolution to act in such a way as to prevent it or combat it effectively.

Frederick of Pinchfield Farm represents Germany, and Pilkington of Foxwood Farm represents England. These two characters, representing countries rather than historical figures, are made as typical as possible — even to their names — so that they have few recognizable individual traits. Pilkington, as England, is described as the typical English "gentleman-farmer" (or a satire on the type), easy-going and a disgracefully bad manager; (England suffered from a depression in the 1930's, which Orwell described in *Wigan Pier*). He passes his time in the sports of fishing and hunting. Frederick is described as a satire on the typical German businessman: ". . . a tough, shrewd man, perpetually involved in lawsuits and with a name for driving hard bargains." Aside from the fact that Frederick runs a more efficient farm than Pilkington, that is all the information given. After this they rarely enter the scene, and are felt as an ominous threat to the Farm. We see Frederick again through the animals' eyes as the enemy who helps Jones attack the Farm in the Battle of the Cowshed, and we hear about him through Squealer's propaganda. When Orwell draws closer to the events of World War II, Frederick takes on more of the historical role of Hitler. We learn that he really does drive a hard bargain, when he swindles Napoleon by paying for the lumber with counterfeit bills; and we see Frederick as the enemy attacking and destroying the windmill with dynamite in the Battle of the Windmill.

Finally, and ironically, we see both these farmers — human enemies become friends — at Napoleon's party in the last scene. In summary, these characters, when they are described at all, are given traditional and typical traits; and more often they are merely seen as a vague and dangerous human enemy.

Mr. Whymper, though not representing a country, does represent a group rather than an individual historical figure. He is the group of people who collaborated after the Revolution to help bolster Russia's economy:

engineers, scientists and businessmen, many of them Americans. Because he is a composite figure, he is also made a typical figure; the solicitor or notary of nineteenth-century England immortalized by Dickens. Whymper is the agent who comes to handle the business of Animal Farm with the outside world, and Orwell makes clear his contempt for Whymper's character and actions. It takes a clever and unscrupulous man to recognize that Animal Farm will need an agent. Orwell describes him as "a sly-looking little man with side-whiskers;" no more information is necessary. Whymper's outstanding characteristic is slyness. Once having been introduced as the go-between, Whymper falls out of sight; except as the unwitting accomplice of Napoleon in fooling the outsiders into believing that Animal Farm has a supply of food.

Literary Elements in *Animal Farm*

Style

George Orwell's writing style reflects the same simple and self-conscious honesty as his own personality. He never allows himself to fall into obscure complexity to get his effects; indeed he never uses effects for their own sake. He says, in the article "Why I Write," that his two main goals are to communicate his political lessons and to achieve an effective literary style; and the simpler and clearer his style, the more effective his lesson. He says that "good prose is like a window pane." For this reason the language of *Animal Farm* is simple and unadorned, and the story is expressed in a straightforward and logical way. Orwell does not write "purple passages," but prefers the effect of understatement; the tone is always carefully controlled.

At the same time as he strives for simplicity of language and expression, however, Orwell makes effective and subtle use of atmosphere, of careful organization for a cumulative effect, and of humor, satire and irony. And he has the capacity to make his concern, anger, and passionate belief shine through his prose, without losing control of the tone.

Orwell's essay on style and language, called "Politics and the English Language," (see Orwell's *Selected Essays*), reveals the rules by which he wrote his books, including *Animal Farm*. In summary, these are:

Never use a metaphor, simile of other figure of speech which you are used to seeing in print.

Never use a long word where a short one will do.

If it is possible to cut out a word, always cut it out.

Never use the passive where you can use the active verb.

Never use a foreign phrase, a scientific word or a jargon word if you can think of an everyday English equivalent.

Break any of these rules sooner than say anything outright barbarous.

In short, he wanted to write prose so clear and simple that it would be impossible to use it to tell lies; so precise that any insincerity and illogical thinking would stand out and be immediately obvious. The result, in *Animal Farm*, is language that can be understood and appreciated by anybody. The style is perfectly suited for the rural setting and the simple-minded animals from whose viewpoint the story is told.

Orwell was very concerned with the effect of language on thought, and he treated words as tools. As he said, "the meaning should choose the word," not the other way around; for language should be "an instrument for expressing and not for concealing or preventing thought." He believed that if we express ourselves vaguely and inexactly, we would begin to think in the same manner. And he believed that of all the democratic freedoms, the freedom to think clearly was the most important, the one upon which all the other freedoms rest. It is for this reason that the title of the above-mentioned essay is "*Politics* and the English Language": our political freedom and institutions are directly affected by the *way* in which we think, speak, and write. This is one of the most important lessons of *Animal Farm*, taught not only by the gradual changing of the Commandments (which gradually destroys the animals' political freedom), but taught also by Orwell's writing style. Not only does he try to teach his lessons as clearly as possible, but he also gives us an example of the kind of clear thinking and writing which will protect our freedom.

Satire and Irony

Satire

    Animal Farm is an animal satire. When we speak about *satire* we are discussing the *form* of a story. Satire is the art of criticizing an object through ridicule and contempt. It normally has a witty or humorous tone, but the humor is used to teach a serious lesson: to point out some problem or evil in the real world. Satire (as Orwell uses it) refers to a form of story-telling which is not realistic but fantastic. It teaches its moral indirectly. Of the many kinds of fantastic means which satirists use, the *animal* satire is a favorite. Instead of speaking directly about human problems, the satirist puts animals into a human situation. This is a situation in which the fantasy and the humor are ready-made; besides, the writer can speak as critically and bitingly as he wishes without having to speak directly.

    There are other reasons for the effectiveness of animal satire. Orwell chose to write *Animal Farm* in this form not only because of the difficulty of making a direct attack on Russia at this time, but also because the interest of an animal story, the humor involved, and the simple form in which he was able to express the political ideas, would all help to entertain and convince his readers. Furthermore, he found it easier to arouse sympathy in his readers for the poor victims of the dictatorship when these victims were defenseless farm animals; and it would be easier to arouse scorn and hatred for the dictators when these were, literally, greedy pigs and ferocious dogs. It is for these reasons that, when Orwell decided to expose Russian Communism, he retold the history of the development of Soviet Russia as the history of a fictional community of animals: in other words as an animal satire.

    There are several problems involved in writing animal satire, and in *Animal Farm* Orwell solves them successfully. The animals must always remain recognizably animals — they should not appear as humans disguised as animals. For this reason, Orwell, in the first scene of the book describes the animals characteristically: the hens perching on the rafters, the cows chewing cud. In fact, Orwell's lesson depends in part on reproducing realistically the suffering of ordinary farm animals — so that their desire to revolt should be understandable: as Old Major complains:

> No animal escapes the cruel knife in the end. . . . You, Boxer, on
> the very day that those great muscles of yours lose their power,
> Jones will sell you to the knacker, who will cut your throat and
> boil you down for the foxhounds.

The horses in the story pull loads, the cows must be milked, the pigs remain piggish. Furthermore, the ironic ending which Orwell planned made it necessary for the real animal qualities of the characters to be stressed, so that the final transformation of the pigs to human is a shock — a shock which illustrates that power corrupts the leaders of the rebellion and makes them exactly like the masters against whom they originally revolted.

At the same time as Orwell must create convincing animals, he must also use them to illustrate specifically human problems (especially the political problems of the Russian revolution), and he must therefore introduce a fantastic element: the animals think and discuss, carry out a rebellion, manage a farm and build a windmill. Orwell must achieve a neat balance between animal and human characteristics in the inhabitants of Animal Farm. To achieve this balance he adopts the tone of a "fairy-story" (this is the subtitle of *Animal Farm*), in which fantastic things are described as though they were real, and the reader suspends disbelief.

Orwell makes his task easier by choosing human characteristics appropriate to each animal. For example, in the first scene, Clover is a "stout motherly mare . . . who had never quite got her figure back after her fourth foal," and "last of all came the cat, who looked around, as usual, for the warmest place, and finally squeezed herself in between Boxer and Clover; there she purred contentedly throughout Major's speech without listening to a word. . . ." And after the successful revolt, when the animals finally dare to enter Jones' house: "Some hams hanging in the kitchen were taken out for burial. . . ."

Orwell is always adding simple, realistic details of the characters' animal traits to their human characteristics. For example, after telling how Snowball writes the Commandments on the wall of the barn, he adds, "It was very neatly written, and except that 'friend' was written 'freind' and one of the S's was the wrong way round, the spelling was correct all the way through." Again, when Orwell satirizes the Soviet committees into which the Russian people were organized by Trotsky, Orwell gives appropriate names to the committees which Snowball organizes: ". . . the Egg Production Committee for the hens, the Clean Tails League for the cow. . . ." Orwell describes how the cat joins one of these committees, the Re-education Committee to tame wild animals: "She was seen one day sitting on a roof and talking to some sparrows who were just out of her reach. She was telling them that all the animals were now comrades and that any sparrow who chose could come and perch on her paw; but the sparrows kept their distance." Napoleon's heroic names (copies of Stalin's titles) are:

"Terror of Mankind, Protector of the Sheep-fold, Ducklings' Friend. . ." and so on. Orwell gets a certain humor out of the appropriate combinations of animal and human traits.

Satire generally combines several levels of meaning. In *Animal Farm* these levels are found: the animal story; a history of Communist Russia; and a more general political and social discussion about ideals, revolutions, and the abuse of power. All these levels should be kept in mind at once when reading the book, because the levels interact, and each adds meaning to the others.

Irony

Irony, like humor, is one of the methods by which satire communicates its message. The simplest definition of *irony* is the stating of one thing while intending its opposite. The effect of humor is to make us laugh for the sake of laughter. Irony uses wry humor as a weapon, to teach a lesson. A good example of humorous irony is found in the paragraph above, in the description of the cat's dealings with the sparrows. The cat is *apparently* extremely friendly towards the birds; in *reality* her motives are the opposite, and she is using the excuse of the Re-education Committee in order to catch them. There are several ironic lessons here: the general one about instinct overcoming training and laws, and a more specific political one: that individual character must be taken into account as well as abstract theories when political changes are planned.

There are more complex ironies in *Animal Farm*. One central irony has already been mentioned; it is developed throughout the whole book until its climax in the last scene: the transformation of the pigs into humans. This irony depends upon the teachings of Old Major in the first chapter, specifically that men are the real enemies of the animals and the cause of the animals' sufferings — so that animals should never copy any human habits. As Old Major says, "In fighting against Man, we must not come to resemble him. Even when you have conquered him, do not adopt his vices." This is the central rule of the Commandments. Furthermore, the one infallible argument that Squealer offers to satisfy the discontented animals is "Do you want Jones back?" — that is, the animals' suffering under the pigs is necessary to prevent the return of the human oppression. The ironic lesson lies in the fact that Major's teachings are completely falsified: the pigs, the very leaders in the revolt against man, gradually assume more and more human characteristics, both in their luxurious way of life and in their cruelty to the animals. The ironic climax in the last scene is the final transformation of the pigs into humans; the last sentence reads, "It was impossible to say which was which." This irony underlines the fact that the pigs have merely replaced Jones as the exploiters of the animals — the revolution has failed.

A parallel irony, which underlines the same lesson, is contained in the gradual changes in the Seven Commandments which Snowball originally painted on the wall. Orwell intends the reader to be reminded of the Ten Commandments of the Bible, especially the effect of unchanging law which these suggest: law given by God and inscribed in rock. It is because of their supposed unchanging quality that there is so much irony in the small alterations which the pigs make in each of the Seven Commandments. Each small change has the ironic effect of turning each rule into its opposite. The first Commandment to be transformed stated ''No animal shall sleep in a bed;'' when the pigs move into the house, they add: ''. . . *with sheets*.'' The next is the rule ''No animal shall kill any other animal;'' after Napoleon holds the trial and executes the animals, this is added: ''. . . *without cause*.'' Then, to the rule, ''No animal shall drink alcohol,'' is added: ''. . . *to excess*,'' after the pigs acquire a taste for whiskey. The summary of the first two Commandments, ''Four legs good, two legs bad,'' is changed when the pigs begin to walk on their hind legs: ''Four legs good, two legs *better*.'' The most chillingly ironic change of all (and the one for which Orwell is famous) is that made in the last chapter to the Commandment reading, ''All animals are equal.'' The triumphant new dictator-pigs add: ''. . . but some animals are more equal than others.''

The only one of the Seven Commandments which has not been broken and transformed by this time is the one reading ''No animal shall wear clothes.'' The pigs do not even bother to rewrite this Commandment on the wall.

At this point, ''. . . it did not seem strange . . . not even when the pigs took Mr. Jones' clothes, Napoleon himself appearing in a black coat, ratcatcher breeches, and leather leggings, while his favorite sow appeared in the watered silk dress which Mrs. Jones had been used to wear on Sundays.'' This humorous sight has its most sober ironic overtones — the animals are not so silly as they appear on the surface. Ironically, in reality they already *do* resemble Jones and the other humans more than animals. It is only a week before the final party at which the complete transformation to humans takes place. This irony thus illustrates the serious lesson beneath satire.

There is no rule against humans appearing in animal satires, as long as they do not play a central role. Jones, Frederick, Pilkington, and their various assistants remain in the background. When they do appear, they are not described in any detail; the story is never told from their point of view. Thus, *Animal Farm* fulfils the condition of an animal satire that all the main characters are animals.

Utopia

Animal Farm is a satiric utopia. *Utopia* is a Greek word whose literal meaning is ''no-where,'' but which has come to mean the description of an ideal society, since Thomas More wrote a book about a fictional ideal commonwealth called *Utopia*. Since that time there have been many sincere utopias, all of which have this in common: they are descriptions (social, economic and political) of perfect societies, written for the edification of the author's own countrymen and the improvement of his own society. That is, the utopia always tries to teach a lesson about the real world in which the author lives.

It is a short step from the sincere utopia to the satiric utopia. If the sincere utopia criticizes society by comparing it with an imaginary and ideal world, then the satiric utopia can make just as effective a criticism of society by paralleling it with an imaginary but *imperfect* world. A satiric utopia, then, is a fantastically disguised copy of the real world.

There is often a further ironic lesson in the satiric utopia: a criticism of sincere utopias themselves. That is, a criticism of the excess of idealism in sincere utopias, or in political theories such as Marxism. Such ideal beliefs lead to the naïve faith that paradise can be achieved on earth. A satiric utopia is, therefore, also a satire on abstract theory, which does not take the individual into account.

In *Animal Farm*, Orwell creates a typical utopia. That is, he goes to great lengths to describe in detail the social, economic and political life of the society of the animals. At the same time, *Animal Farm* is a satiric utopia. In this book, Orwell satirizes the sincere utopia by showing the failure of the animals' dream of an ideal society. He satirizes abstract utopian theorists as well, by the depiction of Old Major, who has only one naïve solution to the ills of the animals — the expulsion of the humans. Orwell makes it clear even at the beginning that the problem is not so simply solved: there must be a place for individual differences. This is Orwell's reason for including in his first description of the animals both that lazy opportunist, the cat, and the vain and easily swayed Mollie, the mare, as well as the more co-operative and sympathetic animals like Boxer. The selfish individualism of Napoleon is more ominous, and is the direct cause of the failure of the utopian revolution.

Orwell's lesson in his satiric utopia might seem very pessimistic. He does not mean to say, however, in *Animal Farm*, that all utopian ideals will necessarily fail; nor does he mean to say that all revolutions will necessarily fail. He wants to warn that ideal and abstract — utopian — solutions to political and economic problems must be tested on individuals in practice. And he teaches that flawless societies cannot be built with flawed individuals. Therefore, he indicates, there must be some unchanging moral law — such as the Seven Commandments — by which to guide our actions.

Point of View

The story of *Animal Farm* is told in the third person, and the author does not intrude his own personality into the story. Nor do we enter into the minds of either Napoleon or any other pig or human in the story. The point of view is always the naïve one of the poor farm animals. This point of view is introduced by Old Major himself. He says, for example, of the cows: "How many thousands of gallons of milk have you given during this last year? And what has happened to that milk, which should have been breeding up sturdy calves? Every drop of it has gone down the throats of our enemies.'' By limiting the point of view in this way, Orwell retains an element of surprise, and deepens our sympathy for the animals, by revealing the successive plots of the pigs as these working beasts slowly become aware of them. The reader, on the other hand, can understand clues to the truth which the animals cannot — and through this dramatic irony readers are shocked and frustrated, and are able to identify with the poor animals.

One example of this process is the scene in which Squealer is found lying stunned on the ground beside a broken ladder beneath the wall on which the Seven Commandments are written. "None of the animals could form any idea as to what this meant, except old Benjamin, who . . . would say nothing." Most of the animals do not understand that this scene is proof that Squealer has been transforming the Commandments; but the reader *does* understand, and feels frustration and sympathy. In this way we are carried along from the point of high ideals and hopes at the start, to the shock of final understanding at the end, when the farm animals peep into Jones' house. It is through their eyes that we see that the pigs have changed into humans. But though the animals are confused by this sight, the reader understands clearly the implications of this final scene: that the revolution has come full circle, back to the time of Jones himself.

Atmosphere

The atmosphere of a book can be an important weapon of the author in making us sympathize with his lesson. The *atmosphere* is the mood of a book, which leads us to accept the interpretation of events and characters which the author suggests. Often, the atmosphere or mood is set at the beginning of a work (such as the ominous atmosphere in the first scene in *Hamlet*, on the battlements of the castle), and the reader accordingly expects the events which follow, applying the suggested mood to those events. Orwell tries something slightly different in *Animal Farm*. The lesson of this book centers around the expectations of the animals about an ideal society, and the progressive disappointment of these expectations by the pigs, as the ideal society is destroyed. To parallel this change, Orwell opens *Animal Farm* in an optimistic mood: the tender scene of the animal fable, in which, as well, Major describes an exciting prospect for the animals. Orwell reinforces this mood by the description of the good-natured and sympathetic relations between the animals: Boxer and Clover enter the meeting-place, "walking very slowly and setting down their vast hairy hoofs with great care lest there should be some small animal in the straw.'' Clover, the "stout motherly mare,'' plays foster mother to the brood of ducklings. Above all, Major's speech recounting his vision of the future, and his song, "Beasts of England,'' are optimistic. The scene ends with the animals energetically singing the song "right through five times in succession, and [they] might have continued singing it all night if they had not been interrupted."

This energetic and positive mood is gradually dissipated after the Rebellion, as the difficulties of the animals become progressively worse, and as their Leader becomes more and more cruel and selfish. A good illustration of the progressively darkening mood is found in Orwell's descriptions of the three battles with the humans. The first skirmish, when the animals rebel, is relatively light-hearted: the humans run away without too much fuss, "after only a moment or two" of "being butted and kicked." The second fight, the Battle of the Cowshed, is more ominous, for the men come back with guns, and the only thing that frightens them away is the sight of a stableboy lying apparently lifeless on the ground; they are "gored, kicked, bitten, trampled on." There is no loss of life, however (except for one sheep), though Snowball is wounded. The third fight, the Battle of the Windmill, near the end of the book, is the most frightening of all. The humans use their guns this time, and the animals are chased into hiding. Then the humans blow up the windmill and, though this stimulates the animals to repulse them, several animals are killed. The humans suffer casualties as well: "Three of them had their heads broken by blows from Boxer's hoofs; another was gored in the belly by a cow's horn. . . ." The progressive cruelty of the battles parallels the growing inhumanity and loss of hope in Animal Farm.

Just as the three battles with the humans record the progressive darkening of the mood and atmosphere, so do the various assemblies of the animals help to record it. The first meeting (and its optimistic and energetic mood) has been described: in fact, the whole book, as we have mentioned, moves in a descending line from that initial scene. The next important meeting in that line is the assembly called to decide on the windmill, in Chapter 5. This meeting is the critical point in the change of mood: the atmosphere of the animal fable is lost for good, when the rivalry between Snowball and Napoleon turns ugly. Napoleon suddenly calls his bodyguard of nine fierce dogs (who are the puppies whom he has raised), and chases Snowball from the Farm. The tone of the chase suggests what is to come: for the first time, bloodshed.

The forecast of bloodshed at the hands of the dogs soon is fulfilled. Napoleon calls yet another important meeting, and this one is the opposite of the one called by Major, both in meaning and in atmosphere: it is a trial, at which the rebellious animals are, one by one, condemned and executed. The atmosphere is one of fear: "the nine huge dogs . . . uttered growls that sent shivers down the animals' spines. They all cowered silently in their places, seeming to know in advance that some terrible thing was to happen." Sure enough, "the dogs promptly tore the throats out" of the rebels. The details of the rest of the scene recall the details of Major's meeting. Clover recalls that first meeting now:

As Clover looked down the hillside her eyes filled with tears. . . . These scenes of terror and slaughter were not what they had looked forward to on that night when old Major had first stirred them to rebellion.

And, to reinforce the memory (and the *change* of atmosphere), the animals begin to sing "Beasts of England," (the song they had sung joyfully at the earlier meeting, five times in succession). This time, "they sang it three times over — very tunefully but slowly and mournfully, in a way they had never sung it before." It is the last time the animals are to sing the song, for Squealer announces at that time that this song has been replaced by another. The contrasts in mood are obvious.

The scene is the climax of terror, and from this point the mood of terror lessens. There is no return, however, to the optimism of the early scenes; instead there is a growing mood of despair and resignment: ". . . the habit, developed through long years, of never complaining, never criticizing, no matter what happened." It is in this mood of ignorance and despair that the book ends. The last assembly of the animals comes in the last scene of the book. It is not called — at least, the animals are not called to it. It begins as an exclusive party, for the six most important pigs and the neighboring humans. Led by Clover, the animals find their way into the farmhouse yard, and stare in at the party. The scene is symbolic: the working animals are, literally, as well as socially and economically, on the outside, looking in. Eventually, "the animals crept silently away," in their despairing mood, for the revolution and utopia promised in Major's meeting have been completely destroyed. The mood-changes parallel this destruction.

Structure

The *structure* of a work is the overall design, or organization of the form of the work. It is not necessarily a logical organization, but it is a *balanced pattern*. The plot of *Animal Farm*, as we have seen, follows the history of Soviet Russia; but the chronological order of this history is sometimes changed, to adapt it to the symmetrical structure of the story. Orwell uses symmetry and balance in *Animal Farm* not only for artistic effect, but to emphasize his lessons.

The overall form of *Animal Farm* follows the pattern of an upward movement, then a long downward slope, back to the original position. It has been mentioned in the section on satire that the irony of the animals' revolution is that it achieves nothing, and that the animals find themselves at the end in the state they had been in before the revolution. This irony is followed by the overall pattern of the book: from the high hopes at the start which lead to the successful revolt and the first positive period; up to the critical point when Napoleon banishes Snowball and takes control; then down through the progressive betrayal of the rebellion, to its final failure when the pigs become human.

Within this overall structure there are many internal patterns and balances (between positive and negative aspects) which contribute to the overall symmetry and to the irony of the lessons. Some of these internal balances have already been mentioned: for example the balance between each positive Commandment and its altered, negative version. Again, the ideals in Old Major's speech at the beginning are, one after the other, betrayed by the pigs; while the organization of the society based on Major's ideas takes on just the form which Major had condemned.

A closely related balance is shown in two scenes, both taking place on a hill overlooking Animal Farm. The first of these occurs just after the successful revolution:

> A little way down the pasture there was a knoll that commanded a view of most of the farm. The animals rushed to the top of it and gazed round them in the clear morning light. Yes, it was theirs! In the ecstasy of that thought they gambolled round and round, they hurled themselves into the air in great leaps of excitement. . . .

The scene expresses their pride and optimism in the new society. The second of this pair of scenes takes place after the executions of the animals during Napoleon's trial:

> When it was all over, the remaining animals . . . crept away in a body. They were shaken and miserable. . . . They had made their way on to the little knoll where the half-finished windmill stood, and with one accord they all lay down as though huddled together for warmth.

This perfectly balanced scene underlines the failure of their hopes.

For another such balanced pair of scenes, look first at the scene in which Boxer is described. In his full power he carries on the work of building the windmill almost single-handed:

> Nothing could have been achieved without Boxer, whose strength seemed equal to that of all the rest of the animals put together. . . . Clover warned him sometimes to be careful not to overstrain himself, but Boxer would never listen to her.

This scene should be compared with the later scene in which Boxer attempts to carry on in the same way, despite his failing health:

> Boxer worked harder than ever. . . . In nothing that he did or said was there any sign that his strength was not what it had been. It

70

was only his appearance that was a little altered. . . .

Sometimes on the slope leading to the top of the quarry, when he braced his muscles against the weight of some vast boulder, it seemed that nothing kept him on his feet except the will to continue.

The once-powerful Boxer will soon fall, never to regain his health.

The events surrounding his death provide yet another balance. The first element in this balance is Major's description of Boxer's expected fate under Jones (in Major's speech). Boxer can hope for nothing more under *human* dominion than to be sold after his strength fails, and to be killed by the knacker and boiled down. In fact, this is exactly the fate he suffers under the *pigs*: underlining yet again that the pigs are no different from Jones.

There are many more such balances and patterns. They not only give literary satisfaction, but help to enforce Orwell's lessons.

Plot

The plot of *Animal Farm* more or less follows the history of Soviet Russia, from the days before the Revolution to the time of Orwell's writing, but the chronological order of this history is compressed and sometimes changed to adapt it to the demands of the structure. In addition, some incidents are given perhaps more emphasis than a historian would recommend, while others are glossed over or ignored completely. Again, the reason for these changes is the demands of the structure, as well as the animal-fable form.

The plot is managed in a straightforward fashion. Orwell uses scenes plus narrative passages to move the story along and, as in conventional novels, he often foreshadows later actions. The combination of a fairly simple plot line and plausible characterization of the animals results in a deceptively simple book and is certainly part of the reason it has such a direct impact on the reader.

Some incidents that are important to the plot are treated with deliberate, ironic understatement. For example, after Napoleon purges the animals who "confess" to collaboration with Snowball, the true reign of terror is begun by the dogs, the secret police. It is told in a line or so. Orwell describes Squealer going about justifying the new order and notes in an almost incidental fashion, ". . . . the three dogs who happened to be with him growled so threateningly, that [the animals] accepted his explanation without further question." Other scenes are treated very briefly for the sake of contrast. The actual Rebellion is pivotal to the action but is described in much less detail that the Battles of the Cowshed and the Windmill. The revolt is handled in this fashion to make the point that accident, more than choice, brought about the founding of Animal Farm.

Also worth noting in the plot is the author's use of time factors and devices. The sequence of events is unusually clear. Every time there is a lapse in the narrative, the relationship of the next action is specified: "early in March," "All through that summer," and so on. (A deliberate contrast is provided at the beginning of the last chapter, when we are told simply, "Years passed.") The months and seasons are carefully noted, with particular attention to the details of the farming year — a device that adds to the appearance of realism.

Believability is also increased by the omission of some events that should logically be present. Just as the characters with their combined animal-human qualities are easier to accept because Orwell does not dwell on how they manage to do many things, so the plot is helped by ignoring many improbabilities. For example, there is no suggestion that more humans could be called in to help overcome the rebellious animals; neither are the plans or the building of the windmill completely logical. By avoiding these problems, the author increases the believability of the story and keeps it moving.

Setting

The physical setting of a farm is ideal for Orwell's story. It is appropriate to the pastoral, nostalgic vision of Old Major. Its life is simple in the sense that it is unlike the urban life typical of the twentieth century. It also has the necessary isolation from the world for the birth and development of a new society.

The isolated setting also helps the form of the novel. Satire often uses a closed society — a ship, a spaceship, a farm, a lonely village — to make a simplified description of life more believable. Such a closed society does not come in contact with the rest of the world, so the author does not have to explain its absence.

The setting is ideal for the satire in another way. Because it is pleasant and pastoral, it offers the most vivid possible contrast to the direction the society of Animal Farm takes. Appropriate to Old Major, the setting is inappropriate to the authoritarian society of Napoleon. This is shown especially well in the scene on the knoll after the purge trials, when Clover looks upon the attractive landscape and wonders what has gone wrong in putting Old Major's vision into practice. It is almost impossible for her to believe that in such a place bloodshed and cruelty — man's inhumanity to man, in effect — could become a part of day-to-day life.

That the story should be set in England, like *1984*, is significant. Orwell was never mysterious when he had something to say to his fellow man. As in the later novel, he is saying: it could happen here.

Symbolism

Orwell uses a number of symbols in the novel as part of the mechanism of his satire and as a way of embodying the ideas he intends to communicate. Some are related to human beings and the evil they represent to the animals: the house, whips, and walking on two legs. At first, these symbols are associated solely with Jones. But when the pigs adopt them at the end of the novel, they indicate how the pigs have become indistinguishable from the animals' former master.

Other symbols are associated exclusively with life in the society of Animal Farm such as the green flag and the windmill. The windmill, so important in the plot of the novel, has several meanings. At first, it represents, in Snowball's eyes, the kind of success and good life which the animals will make for themselves. Then, it comes to stand for the conflict between Snowball and Napoleon and their factions. Later, it represents the back-breaking labor which Napoleon uses to keep the other animals busy. It also, of course, represents what the animals must defend against the human enemy.

Like any good symbols, those that Orwell uses are, to begin with, natural aspects of the story he is telling. They take on meaning only because they are shown to be important in the reality he is depicting in the novel. To be too obvious and contrived is the sign of poor use of symbolism, which Orwell never falls into in *Animal Farm*.

Selected Criticisms

Whatever you may say about writers — their private lives, their feeding habits or their taste in shirts — you have to admit, I think, that there has never been such a thing as a literature of appeasement. . . .

For literature is concerned above everything else with the accurate expression of a personal vision, while appeasement is a matter of compromise.

Nevertheless, in wartime there has to be a measure of appeasement, and it is as well for the writer to keep quiet. He must not give way to despondency or dismay, he must not offend a valuable ally, he must not even make fun. . . .

It is a welcome sign of peace that Mr. George Orwell is able to publish his 'fairy story' *Animal Farm*, a satire upon the totalitarian state and one state in particular. I have heard a rumour that the manuscript was at one time submitted to the Ministry of Information, that huge cenotaph of appeasement, and an official there took a poor view of it. 'Couldn't you make them some other animal,' he is reported as saying in reference to the dictator and his colleagues, 'and not pigs?'

For this is the story of a political experiment on a farm where the animals, under the advice of a patriarchal porker, get organised and eventually drive out Mr. Jones, the human owner. . . .

It is a sad fable, and it is an indication of Mr. Orwell's fine talent that it is really sad — not a mere echo of human failings at one remove. We do become involved in the fate of Molly the Cow, old Benjamin the Donkey, and Boxer the poor devil of a hard-working, easily deceived Horse. Snowball is driven out by Napoleon, who imposes his solitary leadership with the help of a gang of savage dogs, and slowly the Seven Commandments become altered or erased, until at last on the barn door appears only one sentence. 'All animals are equal, but some animals are more equal than others.'

If Mr. Walt Disney is looking for a real subject, here it is: it has all the necessary humour, and it has, too, the subdued lyrical quality he can sometimes express so well. But is it perhaps a little too real for him? There is no appeasement here.

Graham Greene, 1945.

In a world choked everywhere with suffering, cruelty and exploitation, . . . Mr. Orwell's Devils have been numerous and, since he is a man of integrity, he chooses real evils to attack. His latest satire, beautifully written, amusing and, if you don't take it too seriously, a fair corrective of much silly worship of the Soviet Union, suggests to me that he is reaching the exhaustion of idealism and approaching the bathos of cynicism. He began as a civil servant, honestly indignant with the misdeeds of the British Empire as he saw it in the Far East. During the Spanish war, a sincere anti-Fascist, he found, like many others of his temperament, that of all the warring groups the most idealistic and least smirched were the anarchists. The fact that they would infallibly have lost the war while the Republican coalition might, in slightly more favourable circumstances, have won it, did not affect his onslaught. At the outset of the World War he repented his past. Realising that Nazi Germany was now an even worse enemy than the British Empire or the Negrin Government, he wrote denouncing the Left. . . . Now that Germany is defeated, it seems almost accidental that his righteous indignation is turned not, say, against the Americans for their treatment of Negroes, but against the Soviet Union. In Stalin he finds the latest incarnation of Evil.

There is plenty in the U.S.S.R. to satirise, and Mr. Orwell does it well. . . . We all know of the sheep, who drown discussion by the bleating of slogans; we have all noticed, with a wry smile, the gradual change of Soviet doctrine under the pretence that it is no change and then that the original doctrine was an anti-Marxist error. (The best thing in Mr. Orwell's story is the picture of the puzzled animals examining the Original Principles of the Revolution, and finding them altered: 'All animals are equal,' said the slogan; to which is added, 'but some are more equal than others.') The falsehoods about Trotsky, whose part in the revolutionary period, only secondary to Lenin's, has been gradually erased from the Soviet history books, is another fair count against Stalinite methods. The story of the loyal horse who worked until his lungs burst and was finally sent off to the knackers' yard is told with a genuine pathos; it represents a true and hateful aspect of every revolutionary struggle. Best of all is the character of the donkey who says little, but is always sure that the more things change the more they will be the same, that men will always be oppressed and exploited whether they have revolutions and high ideals or not.

The logic of Mr. Orwell's satire is surely the ultimate cynicism of Ben, the donkey. That, if I read Mr. Orwell's mind correctly, is where his idealism and disillusion has really landed him. But he has not quite the courage to see that he has lost faith, not in Russia but in mankind. So the surface moral of his story is that all would have gone well with the revolution if the wicked Stalin had not driven the brave and good Trotsky out of Eden. Here Mr. Orwell ruins what should have been a very perfect piece of satire on human life. For by putting the Stalin-Trotsky struggle in the centre he invites every kind of historical and factual objection. We are brought from the general to the particular; to the question why Stalin decided to attempt the terrific feat of creating an independent Socialist country rather than risk plunging Russia unprepared into a war of intervention by stirring up revolution in neighbouring countries. Mr. Orwell may say it would have been better if this policy had prevailed, but a moment's thought will evoke in him the brilliant satire he would have written about the betrayal of the revolution, if Trotsky, who was as ruthless a revolutionary as Stalin, had won the day and lost the revolution by another route. This same error compels the reader to ask whether in fact it is true that the Commissar to-day is indistinguishable in ideals and privilege from the Tzarist bureaucrat and the answer is that though many traditional Russian characteristics survive in Russia, the new ruling class is really very different indeed from anything that Russia has known before. In short, if we read the satire as a gibe at the failings of the U.S.S.R. and realise that it is historically false and neglectful of the complex truth about Russia, we shall enjoy it and be grateful for our laugh. But which will Mr. Orwell do next? Having fired his bolt against Stalin, he could return to the attack on British or American Capitalism as seen through the eyes say, of an Indian peasant; the picture would be about as true or as false. Alternatively, there is the Church of Rome, Yogi, or at a pinch, the more tedious effort to help find the solution of any of the problems.that actually face Stalin, Mr. Attlee, Mr. Orwell and the rest of us.

Kingsley Martin, 1945.

Mr. Orwell is a revolutionary who is in love with 1910. This ambivalence constitutes his strength and his weakness. Never before has a progressive political thinker been so handicapped by nostalgia for the Edwardian shabby-genteel or the under-dog. It is this political sentimentality which from the literary point of view is his most valid emotion. *Animal Farm* proves it, for it truly is a fairy story told by a great lover of liberty and a great lover of animals. The farm is real, the animals are moving. At the same time it is a devastating attack on Stalin and his 'betrayal' of the Russian revolution, as seen by another revolutionary. The allegory between the animals and the fate of their revolution . . . and the Russian experiment is beautifully worked out, perhaps the most felicitous moment being when the animal 'saboteurs' are executed for some of the very crimes of the Russian trials, such as the sheep who confessed to having 'urinated in the drinking pool' or the goose which kept back six ears of corn and ate them in the night. . . .

Politically one might make to Mr. Orwell the same objections as to Mr. Koestler for his essay on Russia in *The Yogi and the Commissar* — both allow their personal bitterness about the betrayed revolution to prejudice their attitude to the facts. But it is arguable that every revolution is 'betrayed' because the violence necessary to achieve it is bound to generate an admiration for violence which leads to the abuse of power. A revolution is the forcible removal of an obsolete and inefficient ruling-class by a vigorous and efficient one which replaces it for as long as its vitality will allow. . . . If Stalin and his regime were not loved as well as feared the Animal Farm which comprises the greatest land-mass of the world would not have united to roll back the most efficient invading army which the world has ever known — and if in truth Stalin is loved then he and his regime cannot be quite what they appear to Mr. Orwell (indeed Napoleon's final brutality to Boxer — if Boxer symbolises the proletariat, is not paralleled by any incident in Stalin's career — unless the Scorched Earth policy is indicated). But it is unfair to harp on these considerations. *Animal Farm* is one of the most enjoyable books since the war, it is deliciously written, with something of the feeling, the penetration and the verbal economy of Orwell's master, Swift. It deserves a wide sale and a lengthy discussion. . . .

Cyril Connolly, 1945.

George Orwell, to judge by his writing, is a man, not without imagination, who is never swept away by his imagination. . . . He stands for a common sense and a reasonableness which are rare today, especially when these virtues are removed from the commonplace, as they are in Orwell's case, though not absolutely.

Animal Farm, a brief barnyard history of the Russian Revolution from October to just beyond the Stalin-Hitler pact, is the characteristic product of such a mind, both with credit and discredit to its qualities. It puts an imaginative surface on the facts, but does not go far beneath the surface and shows little in excess of the minimum of invention necessary to make the transposition into an animal perspective. The facts are straight, and all the wieldy ones are there; the interpretation, within these limits, is plain and true. The implicit moral attitude toward the real historical events is one of an indignation that goes-without-saying, opposed to the nonsense and chicanery of Party dialectics, and to what has come to be recognized, to a large extent through Orwell's writing, as the well-intentioned, peculiarly liberal act of submission to the tyrant's myth. At least by implication, Orwell again makes clear in this book his allegiance to an older and more honorable liberalism that still holds as its dearest thing the right to liberty of judgment. Nevertheless, this is a disappointing piece of work; its best effort is exerted somewhere on middle ground, between the chuckle-headed monstrosity of orthodox Stalinism and the stated anti-Stalinist intelligence of long standing which already knows all this and a good deal more besides. . . .

What I found most troublesome was the question that attended my reading — what is the point of *Animal Farm*? Is it that the pigs, with the most piggish pig supreme, will always disinherit the sheep and the horses? If so, why bother with a debunking fable; why not . . . give assent to the alleged historical necessity?

Though Orwell, I am sure, would not seriously advance the badman theory of history, it appears that he has, nevertheless, drawn on it for the purpose of writing *Animal Farm*. There are only two motives operating in the parable (which is already an oversimplification to the point of falsity, if we take the parable as intended); one of them, a good one, Snowball's, is defeated, and the only other, the bad one, Napoleon's, succeeds, presumably because history belongs to the most unscrupulous. I do not take this to be Orwell's own position, for his work has shown that he knows it to be false and a waste of time in historical analysis; it is, however, the position of his imagination, as divorced from what he knows — a convenient ground, itself a fable, to set his fable on. (If Marxism has really failed, the most ironic thing about its failure is that it should be attributed to the piggishness of human nature.) It is at this point that a failure of imagination — failure to expand the parable, to incorporate into it something of the complexity of the real event — becomes identical with a failure in politics. The story, which is inadequate as a way into the reality, also falls short as a way out; and while no one has a right to demand of *Animal Farm* that it provide a solution to the Russian problem — something it never set out to do — it is nevertheless true that its political relevance is more apparent than real. It will offer a kind of enlightenment to those who still need it, say, the members of the Book of the Month Club, but beyond this it has no politics at all.

Another way of making this point is to compare *Animal Farm* with Koestler's *Darkness at Noon*. Rubashov, also faced with the triumph of the pig, at least asks *why* the pig is so attractive, *why* he wins out over the good. This is a question that can no longer be answered by stating *that* the pig wins out. It is a more sophisticated question, for it realizes that the fact of the triumph is already known, and a more important one, for it leads to an examination of the pig's supremacy along two divergent lines, by way of a specific Marxist analysis of history, or a criticism of Marxism in general, both engaging the imagination at a crucial point. But Orwell's method, of taking a well worn fact that we know and converting it, for lack of better inspiration, into an imaginative symbol, actually falsifies the fact; thus over-extended, the fact of Stalinist 'human nature,' the power-drive of the bureaucracy, ceases to explain anything, and even makes one forget what it is to which it does apply. An indication that a middle of the way imagination, working with ideas that have only a half-way scope, cannot seriously deal with events that are themselves extreme. There is, however, some value in the method of *Animal Farm*, provided it is timely, in the sense, not of newspapers, but of history, in advance of the news. But this is to say that *Animal Farm* should have been written years ago; coming as it does, in the wake of the event, it can only be called a backward work.

Isaac Rosenfeld, 1946.

George Orwell's satire on Russian Communism, *Animal Farm*, has just appeared in America, but its fame has preceded it, and surely by now everyone has heard of the fable of the animals who revolted and set up a republic on a farm. . . .

The story is very well-written, especially the Snowball episode . . . and the vicious irony of the end of Boxer the work horse is perhaps really great satire. On the other hand, the satire on the episode corresponding to the German invasion seems to me both silly and heartless, and the final metamorphosis of pigs into humans at the end is a fantastic disruption of the sober logic of the tale. The reason for the change in method was to conclude the story by showing the end of Communism under Stalin as a replica of its beginning under the Czar. Such an alignment is, of course, complete nonsense, and as Mr. Orwell must know it to be nonsense, his motive for adopting it was presumably that he did not know how otherwise to get his allegory rounded off with a neat epigrammatic finish.

Animal Farm adopts one of the classical formulas of satire, the corruption of principle by expediency, of which Swift's *Tale of a Tub* is the greatest example. It is an account of the bogging down of Utopian aspirations in the quicksand of human nature which could have been written . . . about one of the co-operative communities attempted in America during the last century. But for the same reason it completely misses the point as a satire on the Russian development of Marxism, and as expressing the disillusionment which many men of goodwill feel about Russia. The reason for that disillusionment would be much better expressed as the corruption of expediency by principle. . . .

Official Marxism today announces on page one that dialectic materialism is to be carefully distinguished from metaphysical materialism, and then insists from page two to the end that Marxism is nevertheless a complete materialist metaphysic of experience, with materialist answers to such questions as the existence of God, the origin of knowledge and the meaning of culture. Thus instead of including itself in the body of modern thought and giving a revolutionary dynamic to that body, Marxism has become a self-contained dogmatic system, and one so exclusive in its approach to the remainder of modern thought as to appear increasingly antiquated and sectarian. . . .

A really searching satire on Russian Communism, then, would be more deeply concerned with the underlying reasons for its transformation from a proletarian dictatorship into a kind of parody of the Catholic Church. Mr. Orwell does not bother with motivation: he makes his Napoleon inscrutably ambitious, and lets it go at that, and as far as he is concerned some old reactionary bromide like 'you can't change human nature' is as good a moral as any other for his fable. But he, like Koestler, is an example of a large number of writers in the Western democracies who during the last fifteen years have done their level best to adopt the Russian interpretation of Marxism as their own world-outlook and have failed.

Northrop Frye, 1946.

The basic idea for the story [*Animal Farm*] occurred to him one day in the country when he saw a little boy of about ten years old driving a huge horse along a narrow lane, whipping it whenever it tried to turn aside. "It struck me that if only such animals became conscious of their strength we should have no power over them; and that ordinary people exploit animals in much the same way as the rich exploit the proletariat."

A simple idea, which he developed into a short book of not much more than 30,000 words. . . .

The air of blitheness and buoyancy which fills *Animal Farm*, as it does *Homage to Catalonia*, in spite of the depressing theme, suggests that Orwell was still comparatively optimistic when he wrote it. But by comparing the working class to animals, even noble and attractive ones, he implies that they are at an irremediable disadvantage in the class struggle. The animals' difficulty in using tools is emphasized several times in the book; and it is only the clever but repulsive and odious pigs who are able to learn to use a pen, walk on two legs, and pass themselves off as human beings. One is reminded of Orwell's attitude many years earlier, when he returned from Burma at the age of twenty-four: "At that time failure seemed to me the only virtue. Every suspicion of self-advancement, even to 'succeed' in life to the extent of earning a few hundred a year, seemed to me spiritually ugly, a species of bullying."

It will be remembered that *Keep the Aspidistra Flying* was about a young man who held a sort of immature and self-centered version of the above doctrine; and although Orwell himself, having once found a political purpose for his writing, never relapsed into the mood of that early novel, it does appear in *Animal Farm*, and still more in *1984*, that he ceased to rely upon the generous, humane and unambitious instincts — the "crystal spirit" — of the common man as an effective political ally in the struggle against spiritual ugliness and bullying. And from a certain point of view *1984* can be seen as a restatement of the theme of *Keep the Aspidistra Flying* on a more comprehensive scale and with a deeper political and social awareness.

Richard Rees, 1962.

Review Questions and Answers

Question 1.

Describe and illustrate how in the first scene Orwell makes the fantastic situations and characters seem realistic.

Answer

It is important for Orwell to make *Animal Farm* seem convincingly realistic, so that (for one thing) his readers will apply his lessons in real life. For this purpose, Orwell gives much realistic detail in his descriptions of events, and he gives his animal characters recognizably human, realistic personalities.

As for description, the first scene in the book illustrates well Orwell's methods. When the book opens, there is nothing to tell us that this will be a fantastic situation in which animals think, talk and act like humans. We first read about Farmer Jones: the tone is simple and objective, and the description is full of small circumstantial details, such as the fact that he locked the hen house but forgot to shut the pop-holes, that he used a lantern, that Mrs. Jones was snoring in her sleep, and that Jones kicked off his boots at the back door. Orwell thus sets a completely normal and realistic scene.

Orwell then introduces his animal characters, continuing on in the tone he has already set, and giving the same type of realistic details: the pigs come into the barn and settle in the straw, the hens perch on the window-sills, the cows begin to chew their cud. Of course there is a minor shock when we read that these animals are having a meeting; but the realistic tone of the whole description gets us quickly over this difficulty, and we accept the fantastic story as realistic.

The descriptions of the animal characters help to reinforce this realistic effect. The animals have a combination of appropriate human and animal traits. For example, Old Major is described as a Middle White boar whose show name is Willingdon Beauty; he sits in a bed of straw; his tusks have never been trimmed. Mixed in with this realistic animal description, however, are human details, such as the fact that all the other animals respect him, and that he has a wise and benevolent expression; and Major makes a formal speech to the assembled animals, who group themselves around him and sit quietly to listen in a very human fashion.

Boxer and Clover are also described in this scene by a combination of the animal and human. They are distinctly horselike when they enter the barn, moving slowly and heavily on "vast hairy hoofs." Boxer is a huge horse, with a white stripe down his nose. But he is also described as not of first-rate intelligence, and as being respected by the other animals for his steadiness. Clover is a motherly mare who has had four foals; Orwell adds, on the other hand, that she never quite got her figure back after these children. The human characteristic of these beasts fit their animal natures quite neatly.

Benjamin provides a final example of such a description. As a donkey, he is long-lived, and he shows the typical donkey's bad humor and stubbornness. Orwell adds to this the facts that Benjamin seldom talked, and usually only made cynical remarks — which are human traits appropriate to Benjamin's animal nature. Orwell also confides that Benjamin has a devoted friendship with Boxer — yet another human trait.

Question 2.

Describe the causes of the failure of the animals' Rebellion to bring about an ideal society. What lesson is Orwell teaching by this failure?

Answer

The animals' rebellion fails for several reasons. Major has too idealistic and abstract an idea of the perfect society, and he does not explain how it is to be put into practice. It also fails because Snowball cannot compete with Napoleon's brutal and selfish purpose to gain power. Again, it fails because the other animals are either too stupid or too weak to fight Napoleon, or they are too vain and selfish to contribute to their society. society.

Old Major's idea that man is responsible for the animals' condition is too simple, as we discover later. The animals learn eventually that the ordinary hardships of life such as hard work, bad crops, cold winters, continue; and they ultimately learn that even pigs can act as badly as humans. In addition, Major's dream is of the past, a country world in which the animals will have simple comforts and food. Thus, he cannot deal with the future or even the present: he admits that he does not know *how* the change will come about.

One result of Major's vagueness is that the Rebellion comes unexpectedly, without giving the animals the opportunity to work out a really democratic system. On the surface, the new society is free and its inhabitants equal (as the Commandments say), but in reality the pigs immediately take over. This is yet another reason for the failure of the Rebellion: there is such a wide difference between the intelligence of the pigs and the other animals, that the clever pigs begin to control the society without opposition.

This fact in itself would not have necessarily meant failure, but Napoleon, one of the natural leaders of the pigs, is selfish and power-hungry, and he does not waste his efforts on the social projects with which Snowball concerns himself. Napoleon concentrates his energies in winning power. While Snowball organizes the society, Napoleon's only project is to train the puppies whom he has taken from their mothers, so that they will grow into the fierce bodyguard with whom he takes power. When he becomes dictator, he crushes the opposition of those pigs who might have done some good for the society: he banishes Snowball, and he kills the four dissenting pigs. The remaining animals are too stupid to realize what he and the pigs are doing to them.

There are several animals who do nothing to help the revolution, and so contribute to its failure. These are Moses the Raven, the cat, and Mollie. Moses tries to hinder the Rebellion by preaching to the animals that they should concentrate their hopes on Sugarcandy Mountain, where they will go after they die, in preference to Major's paradise on earth. Moses escapes with Jones, but returns later, and continues to preach about Sugarcandy Mountain. He is really a parasite, first on Jones, then on the pigs. The cat is merely selfish, sharing in the advantages of the new society but disappearing whenever there is work to be done. The mare, Mollie, is too vain and stupid to understand that to work for humans is slavery. She never loses her love for the badge of slavery, ribbons, and for lump-sugar. She does as little work as possible, hides during the Battle of the Cowshed, and keeps up her acquaintance with the neighboring humans. Persuaded by her vanity, and some ribbons, Mollie finally deserts Animal Farm.

By showing how the dream of an ideal society fails, Orwell is trying to teach that abstract ideals are not sufficient in themselves to bring about a beneficial change in society. The facts of ordinary life, and of individual differences, must be taken into account.

Question 3.

Describe and compare the characters of Boxer and Mollie.

Answer

Boxer is a patient, relatively unintelligent, faithful animal, working beyond the limits of his strength for the good of the community. Mollie is vain and selfish, but no more intelligent than Boxer; she thinks more of the affection of her human masters than she does of freedom and common sympathy with the other animals. It is ironic that both of these are horses.

From the very first, Boxer is the most faithful of the animals to the teachings of Animalism. Once they understand these teachings, he and Clover pass them on to the other animals. During the Rebellion and the Battle of the Cowshed, Boxer fights bravely, and during the latter battle, it is the sight of Boxer knocking down a stableboy that finally panics the humans, so that they flee. Mollie is never interested in Animalism, nor does she understand its principles, as she shows by asking about the ribbons. Furthermore, she shows her cowardice at the Battle of the Cowshed, hiding at the first sign of fighting.

Boxer labors in the ordinary work of the farm as well as in the huge and difficult task of constructing the windmill. He puts his strength and persistence to best use, and Orwell says that the task would have been impossible without him: he is the backbone of the Farm. He is not discouraged by the destruction of the windmill on two occasions. In the end, he overworks, so as to have the windmill almost completed before he retires; as a result he falls ill and dies. He has sacrificed his life for his comrades. Mollie, on the other hand, works a little as she can, inventing mysterious pains to shirk it. She continues to enjoy ribbons and lump-sugar, and she is discovered by Clover being patted by a neighboring farmer; both forbidden by Animalism. In the end, Mollie deserts Animal Farm and her comrades, and returns to her servile role with men.

Boxer and Mollie show opposite personal qualities, which result in completely different attitudes towards society. Boxer co-operates in the construction and work of society, while Mollie shirks her work. The different fates of these two follow from their characters.

Question 4.

Compare Old Major's dream of a new society at the beginning of "Animal Farm" with Snowball's dream of a society built around the windmill. And compare these two with the society of the Farm at the end.

Answer

In his speech to the animals, Old Major describes a simple, natural country society in which all the animals are free and equal. Snowball describes a society in which the animals live in comfort, by the aid of machines powered by the windmill. The society at the end of *Animal Farm* is the opposite of both of these optimistic dreams: the majority of animals are neither free nor equal, and they live in misery.

Old Major wants to free the animals from human rule, and to give the animals a comfortable standard of living. His idea is a simple, agricultural way of life, living off the produce of the farm: the song "Beasts of England" describes this life. The only "riches" in this song are barley and wheat and other foods for the animals. As Major declares, it is a dream of the *past*.

Snowball tries to convince the animals to vote for the construction of a windmill by describing a world of the *future*, a world in which machines do the work of the animals. The windmill is to be used to run an electricity generator, which will power all the machines on the farm; and also to provide all the artificial comforts such as light, electric heaters and hot water for each animal. The simple natural world of Major's dream has been replaced in Snowball's scheme by a complicated and artificial machine world. And Snowball makes no mention of freedom in his speech.

The world of Animal Farm in the last chapter of the book is unlike either Major's dream or Snowball's vision of a technological civilization. The animals still work hard for their living and they are often cold and hungry. And they are neither free nor equal. The windmill has been built, but it is not used for the animals' benefit, but rather to grind corn so as to make money for the pigs' expensive tastes. The dictatorship of the pigs replaces the former human masters, but aside from this, there is no change at all in the condition of the animals — it is what it had been at the beginning. At the end, the pigs even change into humans, to complete the similarity.

Question 5.

Describe any one passage in "Animal Farm" in which the satire is particularly clear, and explain the satire.

Answer

One passage in which Orwell's satire is quite clear is Old Major's speech to the animals at the beginning of the book. *Animal Farm* is a satire on the history of Soviet Russia, and here Orwell satirizes Communist beliefs. Old Major represents Marx, and his speech is a satire on the principles of Marxism, on which Communism is based. In the satire, humans represent Marx's "capitalists," while animals represent the masses. Thus, where Marx criticizes capitalists as the cause of the workers' sufferings, here Major criticizes humans as the cause of the animals' misery. Once Orwell has chosen the form that the satire is to take, the rest of the passage follows inevitably (and the rest of the book as well). Major describes the animals' wretched existence on a minimum of food, their forced labor, and their slaughter as soon as they grow old or useless. He says the one solution to their problem is to get rid of man. As a result, the animals would begin to enjoy a life of freedom, comfort, sympathy and equality.

The reader sees the application of this description to the condition of the masses (at least, in pre-war days). He also sees the flaws in Major's abstract ideas, because of the simple animal situation described: in fact, though man *is* responsible for their lot, removing man will not solve all the animals' problems. First of all, there remains the necessity of hard work to satisfy their needs (as Orwell shows later); and also, the animals themselves have all the defects of their human masters: cruelty, selfishness, vanity, desire for power.

Orwell neatly summarizes the criticism of Major's abstract ideas by a humorous and ironic bit of action in this passage. At the moment when Major is declaring that all men are enemies and all animals their friends, he is interrupted by the noise of the dogs chasing some rats. The rats may be friends according to Major's principles, but as Orwell shows, satirically, in practice they are still the dogs' prey. This action, typical of the animals and thus understandable, is an example of Orwell's humorous, ironic animal satire, so effective in teaching Orwell's lessons.

Question 6.

Orwell calls *Animal Farm* a fairy story. Can it be read with delight for its own sake, independent of any specific satire of the human world?

Answer

Although *Animal Farm* is an allegory, it has its own intrinsic logic and interest. We may forget, therefore, the human world of politics and history and accept fully the world of *Animal Farm* either on its own terms (that is, as a fairy tale) or as a general satire on human nature and actions. It is staged with an appealing cast of characters; it evolves in suspense and intrigue; there are affecting moments of pathos and compassion, love and sacrifice; there is a compelling climax. Thus, it is hardly necessary to know that Major is a composite of Marx and Lenin or that Napoleon represents Stalin, and so on. These pigs are interesting for their own sake, and not necessarily because they represent historic figures of the real world. We need not think of Boxer in relation to anyone to love and pity him. Benjamin, too, is convincing and interesting in his own right — we are grateful for his company and listen with respect to his remarks.

The story unfolds with clarity and that sense of inevitability which characterizes any work of art. With his nine fierce dogs, we have no doubt that Napoleon will rise to absolute power. The impact is not in what ultimately happens, but in the hooks and turns that follow one from another. Once the pigs begin sleeping in beds, we know they will find cause to violate the other commandments and then fraudulently justify their actions. Orwell balances this inevitability with an artistically deft handling of the circumstances behind the violations.

Animal Farm, then, may be read without knowledge of the human world from which it is drawn. It is a world with its own meaning and excitement, its own charm and beauty, its own evil and hate.

It can also be read as a very nonspecific satire on what people are likely to do in situations involving power. And the fact that it can be enjoyed on these general levels, as well as a comment on Soviet history and on Communism, proves the richness of its many-leveled structure.

Bibliography

Atkins, John. *George Orwell: A Literary and Biographical Study*. London and New York: Frederick Ungar Publishing Co., 1954. The first full-length study of Orwell, by a friend and fellow journalist.

Brander, Laurence. *George Orwell*. New York: Longmans, Green and Co., 1954. A survey of Orwell's work by a BBC colleague. Much used by later scholars though some now question its face-value acceptance of all Orwell's autobiographical statements.

Calder, Jenni. *Chronicles of Conscience: A Study of George Orwell and Arthur Koestler*. London: Martin Secker & Warburg, 1968. A study of the two writers' fight against authoritarian government and social injustices. The material on Orwell emphasizes the use and misuse of language as propaganda and the relationship between conscience and political fact.

Connolly, Cyril. *The Modern Movement: 100 Key Books from England, France and America 1880-1950*. London: Deutsch, A Grafton Book, 1965. Includes brief but excellent descriptions of *Animal Farm* and *1984*. He calls the former the best fable in the English language.

Crick, Bernard. "How the Essay Came to Be Written." *Times Literary Supplement* 15 Sept. 1972. Includes a description of Orwell's own introduction to *Animal Farm*, which was not published with the book and was only discovered in 1971. The article details Orwell's difficulties in getting the book published.

Eliot, T.S. "T.S. Eliot and *Animal Farm*: Reasons for Rejection." *Times* (London), 6 Jan. 1969. The famous poet's reasons for recommending rejection of the novel when it was submitted for publication to Faber & Faber.

Forster, E.M. *Two Cheers for Democracy*. New York: Harvest, 1951. Includes an important early estimate of Orwell.

Greenblatt, Stephen. *Three Modern Satirists: Waugh, Orwell and Huxley*. New Haven: Yale University Press, 1965. A coherent, scholarly analysis of Orwell's work as a whole, emphasizing some apparent contradictions in his thinking and applauding his use of satire.

Gross, Miriam, ed. *The World of George Orwell*. London: Weidenfield & Nicolson, 1971. A collection of eighteen essays; half biographical, half literary. Most are by well-known scholars and are very interesting.

Hollis, Christopher. *A Study of George Orwell*. Chicago: Henry Regnery Co., 1956. A good basic study of Orwell's work, written late enough to achieve some perspective on his politics. Hollis was also one of the first critics to question the accuracy of all Orwell's supposedly autobiographical writing.

Hopkinson, Tom. *George Orwell*. Rev. ed. London: British Book Council, 1965. A much-used pamphlet, but regarded by most critics as superficial.

Howe, Irving. "George Orwell: 'As the Bones Know' " *Harpers* 238

(January, 1969). Reprinted in *Decline of the New*. New York: Harcourt, Brace & World, 1970. A very enthusiastic review of Orwell's ideas and popular influence, with emphasis on his moral force.

___. *Politics and the Novel*. New York: Horizon Press, 1957. Includes an argument that intellectual critics of both the right and the left have tried to diminish Orwell because they cannot face the dire implications of *Animal Farm* and *1984*.

Kalechofsky, Roberta. *George Orwell*. New York: Frederick Ungar, 1973. An account of Orwell's life, works, and character, done very simply — some critics say too simply.

Lee, Robert. *Orwell's Fiction*. Notre Dame, Ind.: University of Notre Dame Press, 1969. An analysis of each of Orwell's novels. Very worthwhile for students.

Meyers, Jeffrey. *George Orwell: 1903-1950: An Annotated Bibliography*. New York: Garland Publishing, 1977. Some 500 entries with evaluations.

___. *George Orwell: The Critical Heritage*. London and Boston: Routledge & Kegan Paul, 1975. Reprints of 108 reviews, from around the world, of nearly all Orwell's works, tracing his reputation from 1933 to 1968. A long introduction covers the dominant themes of the criticism as well as Orwell's career.

Modern Fiction Studies 21 (Spring, 1975): 1-136. A special issue on Orwell with many interesting essays, though none are specifically on *Animal Farm*.

Oxley, B.T. *George Orwell: Literature in Perspective*. London: Evans Brothers Ltd., 1967. An introductory study on Orwell with an especially favorable evaluation of *Animal Farm*.

Powell, Anthony. "George Orwell: A Memoir." *Atlantic Monthly* 220 (October, 1967). A vivid personal sketch of Orwell by a friend and contemporary in British literary circles.

Rees, Richard. *George Orwell: Fugitive from the Camp of Victory*. Carbondale, Ill.: Southern Illinois University Press, 1962. An overall biographical and critical study by one of Orwell's closest friends. It has been much used by subsequent scholars.

Trilling, Lionel. "George Orwell and the Politics of Truth." *Commentary* (March, 1952). Reprinted in *The Opposing Self*. New York: Viking Press, Compass Books, 1955. A very influential essay at the time. It rates Orwell's literary importance as less than do many critics but emphasizes why and how he struck the popular imagination by speaking out on contemporary political life.

Williams, Raymond, ed. *George Orwell: A Collection of Critical Essays*. Englewood Cliffs, N.J.: Prentice-Hall, 1974. Reprints of essays from three "generations" of critics. Some are very valuable and easy to read.

Woodcock, George. *The Crystal Spirit: A Study of George Orwell*. Boston: Little, Brown and Co., 1966. A biography mixed with explication of

Orwell's ideas and work and an appreciation of his style. Many critics feel this is the best full-length study of Orwell.

World Review 16 (June, 1950). A special issue on Orwell, published as a memorial of his death. Contains biographical sketches and essays on his major works.

Zwerdling, Alex. *Orwell and the Left*. New Haven: Yale University Press, 1974. A study of Orwell's political ideas and his search for a literary form in which to express them. Although not all critics agree with Zwerdling's evaluations, his distance from the period gives him a certain advantage over Orwell's contemporaries.

NOTES